3/19

201 PLANS

201 PLANS

TO BUILD
OR REMODEL
YOUR HOUSE

Introduction

Beryl Frank

Weathervane Books
A Division of Imprint Society, Inc.
Distributed by Crown Publishers, Inc.
One Park Avenue
New York, New York 10016

Contents

INTRODUCTION

I. So You Want to Build a House

Part of the American dream is and has been owning your own home. Everybody has dreams about what they want in their ideal home. The do-it-yourself enthusiast has dreams of a complete and separate workshop where he or she can keep all the needed tools and equipment ready for use. Perhaps a wood burning fireplace is the thing you have always yearned for—or maybe you want a house with everything on one level for easy living.

Whatever your particular dream is in regard to the house you want must take careful planning and thought to make that dream a reality. The house that you build to fulfill those dreams is probably the biggest single investment of both money and time you will make in your entire lifetime. Think and plan before you jump into the house market. And above all, to make that dream house really fulfill your needs, consider the requirements of your own family first.

Why Are You Building?

The kind of house you build depends in large part on your own reasons for building. There are many different reasons for moving. The birth of a child may make your present living quarters crowded or you may want to provide more outdoor activities for the family in a suburban area. Three generations living under one roof frequently call for more space and extra rooms for privacy.

An increase in salary can be the reason you are building. The extra money means you can afford more. Perhaps that dreamed-of swimming pool or patio is now affordable. It may even be a desire to be closer to your place of business —or further away—which motivates you to build your own home.

Still another reason for building those dreams can be the approach of retirement age and the shrinkage in the size of the family which this brings. Your space needs have decreased as the children are grown. You no longer need four bedrooms but you still want a home.

Whatever your reasons for building may be, the kind of house you choose must be suited to those reasons. If three generations are sharing one house, the needs of the family are different than the needs of a husband, and wife, no children, who both work. Tailor your house to your needs. That working couple may still want "three bedrooms"—one for sleeping, one for guests and one for a workshop or home office. No builder can tell them what they need. They must decide themselves. So must you.

How Are You Going to Use Your House?

Naturally, your first answer to that question is—"We're going to live there." And of course, you are.

By counting up the family members, you can decide how many bedrooms you will need. That takes care of the sleeping. You can also figure how many bathrooms you want in the new house. If the family all had to line up and wait turns on one another for a single bathroom, you will certainly want to include more than one bath in the new house.

These are some of the decisions you will have to make. And when you get to the financial planning, you may have to make choices as to what is most important. If that extra bathroom is less important than the enlarged family room to you, you may sacrifice the plumbing. But let the choice be yours after you have explored all the angles.

Both your occupation and your hobbies must be considered in relation to your dream house. An artist (either professional or Sunday painter) would want and need space for a studio. An accountant, who either works from home or brings work home, might need space for a desk and file cabinets. A hobby, such as weaving, dictates enough space somewhere for a loom and the creative seamstress needs a sewing corner. If there is that do-it-yourself workman in the family, space must be allotted for a workshop.

How You Live

How you live in your house is an important consideration for the house you build. The family who enjoys formal dinner parties frequently will need an emphasis on the living areas. Space must be allotted for comfortable spreading out so that guests can move around with a before-dinner drink. A small but cozy dining area will not be sufficient for regular and frequent entertaining.

The informal family life-style will have more emphasis on a general family room. This family wants space where young people can stretch out and watch TV or bang on the piano—an all purpose room with comfortable easy chairs. No dainty china ornaments here. Family usage dictates practical child-proof construction.

Adequate space for family needs is certainly a prime consideration when planning your home. But space alone is not the only factor. Good traffic patterns make a dream house a pleasant reality as well.

What Is A Traffic Pattern?

Take a look at the floors in your present home or apartment. Isn't there some stretch of floor which is used more than any other? It could be the walk from the back door, through the kitchen to the bedrooms. The traffic pattern here is where most family members travel in the house. Mother comes in with groceries, shelves the perishables and goes back to her room to change clothes. Father enters and also goes back to change. The children come home from school, drop outer wraps and take books back to their rooms. The traffic pattern here is from the kitchen to the bedrooms.

In planning your new home, traffic patterns may create a need for a foyer and closet near the back or front door (whichever is used by the family). Traffic patterns might dictate the placement of studio or office out of the line of family traffic. Again, your personal family needs must be considered.

At this point, you may be wondering how much family analysis is necessary. The more you know about your personal requirements, the better able you will be to look over plans for building that dream house of yours. And you will be looking at plans—those mysterious paper pictures drawn to scale which are the picture on paper of your house.

The Floor Plans

Anyone can look at a photograph and see what a house looks like. But the person who builds his own house—YOU—may not see that picture. You may have to look at floor plans and from them, visualize what the interior of the house will be like. Can you tell from a blueprint whether a closet is 24 inches deep? Which way does the hinged door on the linen closet swing? Is there space enough in the living room opening for an upholstered sofa to be brought into the room?

These are only some of the things you can learn from floor plans. In deciding the kind of house you need and want, it is a wise idea to look over a lot of plans. Look at everything from the colonial-style traditional 2-story home to a modern rancher. Be familiar with the way plans are drawn up. It will not take long for you to begin deciding what works for you and your family.

An educated buyer is usually a wise buyer. The house you want to build is one of the biggest investments you will make in your entire life. Take the time to learn first. You will avoid costly mistakes later. Ask questions and check out the answers. Learn the difference between a girder and a joist, wallboard and plaster, shingles and siding.

The more you learn and plan, the better able you will be to build your house and end up with the house of your dreams. Well made plans, tailored to your own family needs, will help insure the fulfillment of those dreams.

II. Proceeding to Build

You have now completed your analysis of your needs and looked over enough house plans to know what you want. You may even have that set of house plans, own the lot on which you wish to build and are ready for the next step. There are several things available to you, one of which is whether or not you will use an architect.

The Architect

"Hiring an architect costs money and I don't have any money to waste."

This philosophy may be very true but there are times when it pays to spend more to save in the long run. An architect does charge for his services. In round figures, these charges are around 20 percent of the total cost of construction. For example, in a $10,000 house, the fee for the architect might be $2,000.

The architect in charge of a house looks at that house from the overall picture. He is a trained person who visualizes all aspects of the whole. He sees the house in relation to the lot chosen. He is concerned with the most advantageous way of setting that house on the lot. Such things as the correct exposure for the right rooms are important to him as they will be to you when you live in the house. Perhaps you prefer morning sun to wake up to. The architect will know how best to place the bedrooms to accomplish this for you.

In your kitchen alone, the workmen will include plumbers, electricians, painters, cabinet makers to mention a few. The architect can and does coordinate all of these people and insures that the work done is according to your plans and specifications.

In selecting an architect, choose a registered architect. He may not be Frank Lloyd Wright, but he will be a graduate of a school of architecture who has usually passed a state examination. The letters A.I.A. after his name stand for American Institute of Architects—a national professional association with specified standards and ethics. (All registered architects do not belong to A.I.A. This is a matter of personal choice.)

In short, when you hire a competent architect, you can sit back and relax while your house is being built. The work and responsibility for seeing that it is done right falls on his shoulders, not yours. You will be consulted along the way, but you can rely on the man you are paying to take care of the endless details of building your house from hiring the first contractor to the last of the landscaping. It may be either a luxury or a necessity depending on how much time and know-how you have to give your house.

The Builder

The builder or general contractor for your house can range from a one man operation to a large organization ready to build a total housing community. There are advantages both ways. The one man operation may be able to give more concentrated attention to your house. The large organization, due to multiple buying, may be able to save you money on materials. It is a two sided coin and your decision will be based on what is available where you want to build.

The builder is more concerned with sound construction than an unusual approach which might appeal more to the architect. Where the architect is looking for that special something to look good on the pages of "House Beautiful,'' the contractor leans toward the more conventional.

Do not confuse the builder with the sub-contractors. The plumbers, electricians, etc. are all sub-contractors and it is to the builder that they report. Because the builder regularly uses these independent companies, they will give him better service, as a rule, than they would give you. Your disappointment at a crew not showing up when promised is a one time job. The disappointed builder, on the other hand, may not contract for future business.

The Bids for the Job

The contractor's bid for your job must be specific. It is not enough to say, for example, the bathroom installation will be $2,000. Different fixtures are priced differently and you will be living with those fixtures for a long time. You must know specifics and if there are choices to be made as to color and style, you should make them. You can't build your own house without telling the contractor what YOU want.

Which Contractor to Use

Your choice of which contractor to use should be based on the availability in your area. A satisfied customer living in one of the builder's already completed houses may be the best recommendation to you. Ask the builder to mention some of the homes he has built. Contact the owners and discuss how they liked working with this particular builder. Did he do what he promised to do? Was the work finished in the specified time? Did he come back to correct any mistakes found? These are all valid questions to which you should find answers before you hire a builder.

Your bank or real estate broker may also come up with suggested builders for you. Don't overlook the Chamber of Commerce and the Better Business Bureau. They, too, can make suggestions. You will be working with your contractor for quite a while. It is important to talk the same language. A $500 extra may be small potatoes to the builder whereas it may loom large in your financial picture. Clear communication is important—and equally clear written contracts will avoid much grief.

It is possible for you to be your own contractor. Perhaps, since this is your dream house, this is also your dream. It can be done, but it requires a tremendous amount of time. The professional builder works long hours 5 or 6 days every week. It also requires patience and knowledge. If you are prepared to deal with the sub-contractors, to coordinate their schedules to eliminate conflict, and be on the job supervising every step, go to it. It can be a rewarding experience in the long run. But if this project is less than pleasing to you, find that builder and leave the headaches to him.

Bids for the Contract

Whether you have decided on your builder or are considering several reputable builders, the time has come to accept bids on your house. There are two common types of agreements with builders—cost-plus or lump sum. The cost-plus arrangement means you pay all costs of construction—materials plus labor—plus a stated percentage of them. The lump sum arrangement means the builder gives one figure which includes his cost as well as his profit.

There are advantages and disadvantages to both of these methods. As the person paying the bills, it is up to you to weigh all the pros and cons carefully.

Some contractors feel that working on a cost-plus basis makes their risk less. The contractor can figure more closely what his cost for materials and labor will be and he knows what the agreed profit will be from that plus stated in the contract. The fee is usually 10 to 15 percent of the total cost of the house. This is a nice round profit for the contractor.

A shady builder, however, can always find ways to increase the costs in such an arrangement. It is a strong temptation to the weak to pad payrolls and increase costs—with possible kickbacks from the cooperative supplier—and much money can be added to your costs if you make even a minor change.

If you should decide to add a bulkhead in a family room which was not in the original plans, you will find it includes charges for many different subcontractors. There is more involved here than just the addition of some sheets of wallboard. This of course must be cut to fit the space indicated in the later plans. Cost: one workman's time for cutting and putting it in place. If there happens to be an electrical outlet already installed there (as for a wall clock), an electrician must be brought back to change the wiring. Additional charges by the electrician. While it is hardly likely that you will make such a change after the painting has been done, if this is the case, add additional painting costs. On a cost-plus basis, everyone of the subcontractors will be paid for by you.

The lump sum arrangement will eliminate some of this type of problems. However, in a lump sum bid, the contractor must protect himself. He must figure to absorb any additional costs caused by the unexpected. In this case, the unexpected does not mean your change in the plans. That would be handled separately. It means protection for the builder for any emergencies which may arise. The builder must figure a high bid here in order to be assured of his profit. This is not in any way shady. Rather, it is the necessary profit which the builder has to make to remain in business. It may cost you a little more than the cost-plus arrangement but it can and does work out well in the long run with a reliable contractor.

There is still one more type of agreement which you might want to consider. This is the progressive construction loan. To take advantage of this type of financing, you must own your land free and clear. The land can then be mortgaged and used as security for your construction loan. Money will be paid to the builder in progressive stages. The first payment might be made when the foundation is laid. The second paid out when the house is framed in and so forth. At the completion of each specified stage of construction, the builder will be paid a specified amount of money. This means he is not paying out the total amount and the payments are arranged for with your financing. When the house is completed, final payment to the builder can be made and the rest of your financing will be included in the final papers you sign.

Check over which of these three arrangements will work out the best for you. Weigh all the pros and cons carefully in regards to your personal situation. With careful research on your part as to the builder's integrity, any of these methods will work for you.

Where to Build

The selection of your lot takes you back to questions which only you can answer. Where do you want your house to be? If you are choosing a suburban home, is the location convenient for you to get to your own job? Is there an expressway to town if needed? Are there bus or train facilities? Will you need to be a two-car family with this location?

If you have a young family, available schools must be nearby. Are these schools close enough to be convenient? Is there bus service for a distant school? Do you like the looks of the neighborhood for your growing family? One way to find out more about the school community is to look at the school supply store. What is displayed may clue you in to the type of neighborhood. A good supply of bubble gum can be a healthier indication than ''Mad Magazine.''

You may not want or need a little neighborhood store at the end of the block, but you will surely want to know where the shops and markets you will be using are located. Are they convenient? If it's a shopping center, does it include a bank? Is there a gas station close enough to get your battery started on a cold winter morning? Is there a public library nearby? A drug store?

Not all of these questions will bother you or seem important but they are all worth thinking about. Explore the area you think you want to live in. The more you find out the better able you are to choose wisely.

Building Restrictions

That vacant lot you want to buy may look perfect to you, but don't jump in in a hurry. Find out what building restrictions there are on the property before you put money on the line. Look into the state and local taxes on improved property and make sure you can afford them. Find out if there are assessments on the property such as sewer, street and front-foot charges.

Take a good long look around you. What are the general looks of the neighborhood? Is the condition of the other houses nearby good? Do they seem to be neighbors who care about their homes? Is there a noise factor?—a beltway nearby or an airport or freight trains? Will the noises disturb you when you're living there? All of these are things to be considered when you are purchasing your lot. Trees and landscape may add to the value of your property, but they cannot hide sloppy neighbors. Since you hope to live in this house for a long time, it pays to look now before you leap.

There is one other consideration about the purchase of your site for building. You are just planning this house today, but someday, due to changing family conditions, you may want to sell. Will there be good resale potential here? Think about all of this now, carefully, before you buy.

III. Financing Your House

How Much Can You Afford?

Before you start to look at any real estate, whether it be to start building your house or just looking for land where the dream begins, it is necessary to sit down with pencil and paper. Take a long, hard look at your personal finances. Such things as money for a down payment, money for closing costs and money to meet the monthly payments for your home must be available. The difference between buying a $10,000 house or a $20,000 will be found in your economic picture. Look at that picture long and hard—and realistically.

Some buyers contend it is not the price of the house that matters, but rather the size of the monthly down payments. Since most houses today are bought with some form of mortgage, it is the monthly payments that make the difference.

A good place to begin is with your own monthly earnings. Put that figure down at the top of your page. Do NOT include your wife's earnings if she is under 45. Since she might have to stop work to raise the children, her earning power may be cut and so those monthly payments must come out of your salary alone.

The next thing to figure is the amount of your regular monthly expenses. These include everything you lay out cash for from food and clothing to life insurance, medical expenses and recreation. All of your fixed expenses should be included here.

The formula now is—subtract your fixed expenses from that monthly income. This will leave you the *sum available for housing*. Out of that must come payments for the mortgage, additional costs such as insurance now added, more dollars for heat and air conditioning as well as some reserve for the unexpected repairs and maintenance which may arise.

You are not quite finished figuring. Subtract those extras mentioned above —those additional costs like added insurance, unexpected repairs, etc. from the sum available for housing. You now have a figure which says accurately what you can afford to pay for the loan on your house. Hopefully, now, you will have a large enough down payment set aside in savings to bring your mortgage payments down to the figure you can comfortably manage.

Large or Small Down Payment

The larger your down payment is, the lower your monthly mortgage payments will be. With lending conditions what they are, some advisors tell people they are not buying the price of the house, but the monthly payments instead. It does not matter if the house costs $60,000 if you can get those monthly payments down to what you can afford on your salary.

A large down payment has many advantages. You may find it easier to obtain a loan. You may be able to get that loan at a more reasonable rate of interest. Your total interest expense will be lower. Your equity (that which you actually own and have paid for) in your home will be greater. All of these are valid reasons for making your down payment as large as you comfortably can.

The table below shows combinations of down payments and repayment periods in which you might pay for a $20,000 house at 8% interest.

Effect of size of down payment on cost of $20,000 home, with interest at 8 percent

Down payment	Monthly payment (principal and interest)			Total interest		
	20 years	25 years	30 years	20 years	25 years	30 years
$0	$167	$154	$147	$20,110	$26,280	$32,780
500	163	151	143	19,610	25,630	31,960
1,000	159	147	139	19,110	24,970	31,140
2,000	151	139	132	18,100	23,650	29,500
3,000	142	131	125	17,090	22,340	27,860
4,000	134	124	117	16,090	21,030	26,220
5,000	126	116	110	15,080	19,710	24,580

NOTE: Monthly payment rounded to nearest $1; total interest rounded to nearest $10.

On a 25 year 8 percent loan, every $1,000 of down payment decreases the amount of total interest paid by about $1,130. For example, if you make a down payment of $2,000, the cost of interest over the 25 year period amounts to about $23,650. If you make a down payment of $3,000, the total cost of interest is about $22,340.

But a large down payment may not always be possible. If you are a young family with little cash, you may not have it to put down. Suppose $500 is as large a down payment as you can manage. If you plan to repay the amount borrowed in 25 years instead of 30 years, you will pay about $6,330 less in interest. It is not only the amount of money you put down but also the amount of time you take to repay the loan which can lower the total cost of the loan.

Caution: Do NOT put all of your savings into the down payment. You will need some money for the closing costs on the loan itself. Then, too, there are the expenses of moving as well as some reserve for those unexpected things which always seem to arise. Be prepared for that rainy day when you may have need as well as those monthly payments. Like everything else about your dream house, the mortgage must be tailored to your personal needs and requirements. This applies to the size of your down payment also.

Purchasing the Site for the House

If you already own a plot of land for your house, you won't need to read this section. But if you are still searching for that land, there are several factors to keep in mind. Where you buy is the first thing to consider.

You won't be able to hear the sounds of the country if your lot is in the middle of a city block. By the same token, a rural haven surrounded by forests and fields may not be convenient for you to get back and forth to work. The land, the site for your house, must fit your family needs as well as the house itself.

In looking over land to buy, be sure to consider such practical things as the contour of the land, the drainage, water supply and access to the property. Also, look at the surroundings. What view will you see from the inside of your house? How close will the neighbors be? If possible, see the land in the fall of the year when the leaves have fallen from the trees before you buy. This can save surprises hidden by summer foliage.

When you actually purchase the land, it is a good idea to hire a lawyer. There is much red tape to be unravelled in the purchasing. You will need a survey, a title search and you will need to know if there are any building restrictions as to the use of the land.

A competent lawyer can make this complicated process easier for you. When the deed for the land is drawn up, your lawyer will be sure that your interests are protected. And when the deed is stamped, signed and filed with the proper authorities, the land is yours.

The Sales Contract

You now have your land, your plans, your architect and/or builder and you are ready to move into the next step. This is the point at which you may be asked to sign a sales contract or an agreement to buy. You may be asked to make a deposit.

In this contract, you agree to buy at a stated price, subject to certain conditions.

The agreement should clearly state the purchasing price, amount of cash down payment, method of financing, delivery date of property and delivery of a clear title and survey. Anything to be included as part of the sale from a finished driveway to any promised landscaping should be listed.

The deposit, mentioned above, is sometimes called ''earnest money.'' It is evidence of good faith and the amount can vary depending on the price of the house. The contract should provide for the return of your deposit if you cannot get a loan or if the builder does not comply with the terms of the agreement.

Before you sign any papers in connection with the purchase of your home; READ THEM CAREFULLY. It might be wise for you to get the help and advice of a trained person—again, your lawyer. Some attorneys specialize in this type of work. The cost of consulting an attorney may actually save you money in the long run.

The Mortgage

You have already purchased the land—usually with cash. You are now ready to arrange with a builder for your house. If you have an architect, he will take care of this aspect. If you are working directly with your builder, you will have to decide on the methods mentioned earlier—cost-plus or lump sum. The time has come for you to decide how you are actually going to finance your new house.

There are several ways of financing a house which you are building. Look into all of them to find out which method suits your needs the best and which are available in the area in which you live. Since your mortgage is based on so many individual personal factors, no easy solution as to the best mortgage for you can be offered here. The possibilities open to you in the ways of financing can be presented. The decision as to how you should do it must be up to you.

Construction Loan

A construction loan is a means of releasing money to the builder at regular intervals as he needs it to pay for materials and labor. Some builders cannot afford to lay out all the cash needed to build a house as they go along. This form of mortgage money is frequently supplied to large building firms and developers of multi-housing properties. It is also available to the private individual who is building his own house.

The construction loan which you arrange for at the outset of building your house is only one part of your permanent mortgage. When the work is completed, you will sign final papers. It is at that point that you and the mortgagee, the lender, will state the total amount of the loan, the interest to be paid and the number of years needed to pay off the entire debt.

The Final Mortgage

In plain English, a mortgage is a loan. You are asking someone to lend you enough money to enable you to build and buy a house in exchange for your promise that you will repay the loan in a given amount of time plus the stipulated amount of interest. You are offering the house itself as a security for the loan—i.e. if you default in payments, you will forfeit your house.

There was a time when a man had the needed money to pay cash for his home. If he bought a $10,000 house, he had the $10,000. He then owned his house outright. But in the late 20th century, few of us are able to amass the thousands of dollars needed to buy or build a house. It is common practice today to apply for a mortgage instead.

When you want a loan to buy a car, you naturally turn to your bank. The same can be true when you want a loan for your house. But banks are not the only ones who take mortgages. Financing home loans can come from thrift institutions (more limited as to where they can invest), savings and loan companies, a mortgage company or a mortgage banker. Look around your own community to see what is available to you. Talk to more than one prospective mortgagee. Find out the terms each can offer—and be prepared to discuss your own personal economics. Both parties need to know all particulars to arrange for a mortgage satisfactory to all concerned.

Conventional Mortgage

This is an agreement between lender and buyer. The former will lend the buyer the amount of money needed, using the house as security. This money is to be paid back over an extended period of time with a certain percent of interest due. Home loans can be made for as long as 30 years, although shorter loans can also be arranged.

The only guarantee of payment which the lending institution has with a conventional mortgage is the honesty and reputation of the individual. (No holder of a mortgage really wants a default. Their money and profit come from the interest charged over a period of time.) It is for this reason you will be questioned fully as to the kind of risk you will be. As this is the largest single investment you are likely to make, so this will be your most thorough credit check. It is important and necessary for the satisfaction of both parties.

FHA Loan

Some homes can be purchased by means of an FHA mortgage. This loan means that the Federal Housing Administration will insure the loan when the loan meets the requirements set up by that agency. It is the Federal government's way of making a loan possible with a fairly low down payment and long repayment terms. FHA does not actually lend money. It simply guarantees or stands behind the loan for those qualified.

VA Loan

The VA (Veterans Administration) insured loans came about after World War II. It was intended to allow veterans of that war (and has been expanded to include later wars) to buy housing. The money here is guaranteed by the VA up to 60 percent of the loan for those qualified.

Terms to Know

Before shopping for a mortgage loan, familiarize yourself with the terms of the lending business. Here are some you may run across.

Open-end mortgage—This allows you to borrow more money in the future without rewriting the mortgage. It is a convenient arrangement should you want to repair, modernize or expand your home at some later date. You need to use the arrangement with caution, however, or it can keep you in debt indefinitely.

Packaged mortgage—This covers the cost of household appliances, for example, a refrigerator or a stove; furniture and carpeting along with the house. To include these items in the mortgage may seem like an easy way to acquire them, but it makes them cost more. You pay interest as long as the mortgage runs and they will likely be worn out long before the mortgage is completely paid off.

Prepayment—This permits you to pay off the mortgage before maturity without penalty (a waiting period may be specified). You may find you want to refinance at lower rates or to pay off the mortgage in full before it is due.

Deed—This is a legal paper transferring the title of property from seller to buyer. There are two kinds of deeds—the warranty deed and the quitclaim deed. The warranty deed gives title to the buyer and the seller warrants that he will defend title against any outside claims. If it develops later that someone else still had title to the land or a mortgage claim against it and the sellder did not have a clear title, the buyer may sue the seller for breach of warranty to recover what he paid and to pay for the resultant damages.

The quitclaim deed gives the buyer whatever title the seller may have had and the buyer assumes the risk. A warranty deed is preferred to any other type.

Abstract (or search) of Title—This is a method of checking the safety of the title to a piece of property. It consists of a brief history of the ownership of the property prepared by a lawyer or other trained person. The abstract lists all former transactions affecting ownership, such as liens or claims, deeds, mortgages, sales and any other matter that bears on the title to the property. An abstract makes the buyer reasonably sure that the title is free from defect.

Title Insurance—This is a policy of insurance issued by a title insurance company for a fee. It protects against any title defects. Title insurance gives added protection against outside claimants.

The lender may require title insurance to protect his interest. You, the home buyer, may also want to purchase an owner's title insurance policy for your protection in case a defect in the title develops.

Escrow agreement—This provides that insurance and real estate taxes are to be paid by the lender. The monthly payment is increased by the necessary amounts to pay these costs. If the amount of taxes and insurance changes, an adjustment can be made.

Mortgagee—The person to whom the mortgage is given—that is, the lender.

Mortgagor—The person who mortgages his property, or the borrower.

Closing Costs

The day of reckoning has arrived. The house is finished and the last building truck has left the property. It is time to settle up. All of the concerned parties have arranged a settlement date. You must be aware of what costs are involved at that time of settlement. They are called closing costs.

Mortgage Fee or Broker's Fee

This can be a flat fee ½ of 1% of the mortgage or a straight fee, depending on the customs of specific communities. It pays for such things as money spent by the lender to appraise the value of the house, credit references on the borrower as well as the paper work required to prepare the loan. If these items are not listed separately, there is usually no such fee.

Title Search and Insurance

If you paid for a title search on your lot at the time of purchase (and you probably did) you may not have to repeat this at the final settlement for your house. But a free and clear title to property is protection for both seller and buyer. Some mortgage lenders require title insurance for the property which you, the buyer, may have to pay.

Legal fees

Since settlement for a house is a complicated legal procedure, you may be billed for legal work done by the lender's lawyer. You may want your own lawyer present at settlement. These fees can be moderate or not depending on how complicated your settlement becomes.

There are various other fees which come up at settlement or closing such as the mortgage recording fee, tax money, insurance, etc. To avoid a shock on your closing date, get a list of what your costs will be when you arrange for the mortgage. You may be able to make some changes which will be to your advantage and you will know exactly what is facing you at your final settlement.

Maintenance

When you were compiling your personal financial statistics to find out what kind of down payment you were going to make on this house, there was a caution to remember. Keep enough cash on hand for the unexpected things that come up. Naturally, this applies to unexpected doctor bills and the like. One of the children suddenly needs braces on the teeth. There are always emergencies in any family which require some cash on hand. The same thing is true about your house. Even though you have a loan on which you are paying regularly, there are things that must be considered beyond that.

Utility bills must be paid, of course, but there is also the upkeep of your property. When spring comes, there is a lawn to be tended. This may call for the investment of lawn and garden tools. It costs money to keep up the outside of your home as well as the inside.

Periodically, there are repairs to be made. Such things as new draperies may be put off until the time is right and the money saved, but painting needs to be done regularly to protect your investment in the house. You will need cash on hand for these things. Don't overlook this need in the overall planning.

Insuring your Home

Along with the general maintenance of your house, there is a need to protect your house as well as your personal property. There are various kinds of insurance policies which can help you to accomplish this end. To help you decide on the kind and amount of coverage to have on your home and its contents, discuss your situation with a qualified insurance agent in your area.

Be sure to ask about the cost of different policies. Then you can select the policy or policies that best suit your needs at the least cost to you. There are several kinds of insurance available. Look into them all before you make a final decision.

Fire Insurance

A standard fire insurance policy protects you against losses from damage caused by fire and lightning on the house or structure itself. Fire insurance can be extended to protect against losses caused by hailstorm, tornado, wind, explosion, riot, aircraft damage, vehicle damage and smoke damage. This is known as extended coverage. The extra protection of the expanded coverage may be well worth the additional cost.

Personal Liability Insurance

This policy may be desirable as well as fire and extended coverage insurance. With a liability policy, you are protected in the event someone is injured on your property. Injuries or damage resulting from activities of members of your family are also covered. Some policies have special provisions to pay medical costs within certain limits regardless of your liability.

Theft Insurance

This policy protects your personal property against robbery, burglary or larceny. These policies vary widely. It is, therefore, important to select a policy carefully and to be sure the policy insures against the conditions you want it to. You can obtain a policy in a broad form that protects your possessions both in the home and away from the home but it costs more than the limited form.

Homeowners Policy

This combines insurance on the house, garage and other buildings and on personal property with personal liability. You can buy a homeowners' policy for less than coverages bought separately. Insurance companies usually have more than one homeowners' policy to choose from. The policies differ in the extent of the coverage.

Extra Life Insurance

Sometimes, this is carried on the head of the family to make sure there will be money to pay off the mortgage should he or she die or become disabled before the loan is paid. There are special policies for this purpose. You will want to investigate the cost of this type of policy, especially before deciding whether or not to have the extra protection. What you decide is an individual family matter and will depend on your own particular situation.

IV. Which Style House

Before you can intelligently decide on the house which will become a home for you, it's a good idea to take a look at the various types of houses available and being built on today's market. Until you know the advantages and disadvantages of the different style houses, you cannot choose what will be best for you and your family. Most farsighted buyers do enough looking first to be able to spot easily the difference between a ranch style home, a split level, the story and a half and the conventional 2-story house.

Begin your education in housing on a Sunday afternoon drive around the neighborhood you think you like. Go in and out of housing developments with an open mind. Make notes as you go along and keep on looking. You may spend many Sunday afternoons profitably if you list the things you do and do not like about particular styles of housing. The more you learn, the better able you are to make an ultimate choice which is right for you and your family.

The Ranch House

This house has many names. It is known as a ranch house, a rancher, a one story house. The main thing about this style of house is that it is all on one level.

The one level house is good for young married couples with or without small children. It is also good for older people whose family have dwindled or who are retired. It is a house essentially without steps, although ranchers are made with and without basements in different parts of the country. This lack of steps to climb has decided advantages for small children and older people who may have physical problems with climbing steps.

The maintenance of the ranch house may be less than its 2-story counterpart but the initial cost of building may be more. There is a larger foundation to be dug as well as a bigger roof necessary to cover the one level house.

The size of the lot for the rancher may need to be bigger than that of other homes. The ranch house stretches out to cover more land. A fairly level lot is suggested so that this low to the ground home will actually open its doors at ground level rather than having outside steps to climb.

While a 3 bedroom ranch house may be snug and cozy when the children are little, a careful planner for the future will keep in mind growing needs. The ranch house can usually be expanded at a later date with comparative ease if there is room allowed on the lot for such expansion. That extra wing can be added or simply that large family room when such additions are allowed for. Where there is a full basement unfinished in a ranch house, this can provide space for future expansion.

The ease of upkeep and maintenance on a ranch house have made this a popular style of house all over the United States. There are no steps to climb and because the house is low to the ground, there is a happy combination of indoor and outdoor living.

The Split Level

This style of house has a multitude of names ranging from raised rancher to split foyer to split level, tri-level or bi-level. Whatever its name, this house does have steps on the inside. There are at least two main floors—one or both of which may have access to outdoors, depending on the slope of the lot on which the house is built. However, this is not a conventional 2-story house.

As one name for the house implies, the entrance to the split may be a foyer with steps going up to the bedrooms and down to the living rooms. If it is a tri-level house, the room arrangement might be the same foyer entrance with living room, dining room and kitchen on that level; bedrooms on the upper level; family room and utilities on the lower level. It is possible in a split to have more privacy than in a one level house although there are steps to walk to accomplish this.

The split level house is particularly well adapted to a sloping lot. The lower level is usually set into the ground on what may be called a basement level. But that lower level is planned and utilized for family living. This is where informal decor is frequently used with attractive panelling to make up for the lack of large windows. The upper levels can be zoned with bedrooms off to themselves.

The completed split offers more living area than its rancher counterpart but it can be difficult to build. It may require complex bulldozing and grading and may present problems with heating and air conditioning. Both the upper and lower levels need extra insulation to keep them comfortable in summer and winter.

Although there is more living space in a split, there are also those steps. Anyone coming into the house usually has a few steps to walk—not a full stairway as in the 2-story house—but at least three to five steps up or down. If steps present a problem for your family, this is not the house for you.

But if you have a sloping lot and want a house which can be integrated into the landscape surrounding it, the split level, in one of its many forms, may be ideal for you.

The Story and a Half

This house also has several names in different parts of the country. It is called a Cape Cod house, a bungalow or a story and a half. It is a classic

American house with a great deal of charm and several economic drawbacks as well. It is not used as frequently today as it was many years ago but it might just be what you will need.

The story and a half costs almost as much to build as a full 2-story house without offering as much living space. But this is a house which can be expanded later on. The unfinished attic of the story and a half can be made into extra rooms years after the house is built. This is an ace in the hole for the young family just starting out. The first floor is complete with one or two bedrooms. Later on, when need arises, the attic rooms can be improved for use.

Whether or not the attic rooms are to be improved at the time of building, it is a wise planner who will have plumbing lines roughed in. It is easier to do this during construction than later on.

The typical Cape Cod has a rather steep pitch to its roof. This is why there is space for those extra rooms. But this area, being directly under the roof, tends to be hot in summer and cold in winter. Sufficient insulation can overcome this problem. While dormer windows may not be in keeping with strict Cape Cod design, they do allow more air and light into what could otherwise be a dark area.

Since there is at least one bedroom on the main floor of a story and a half house, this is the kind of house which can expand for family living and contract, by closing off the upstairs rooms, when children have grown up and gone their own way. It is then as convenient as the ranch style with all living on one level —and that level offering easy access to the garden or patio.

The 2-Story House

The 2-story house is often referred to as a colonial house—but don't let the name fool you. It is not the same as early American by any means and adapts itself well to a variety of sized lots. It looks good on either a small piece of land or on a large wooded area and offers the best building value per square foot of living space of any of the other types of housing. It offers double the amount of living space as a ranch house with the same sized foundation and roof.

Of course, you cannot have a 2-story house without a full set of stairs to climb. This is no problem when the entire family is hale and hearty but it can be wearing when there is a case of chicken pox in bed upstairs and the kitchen is down. It can be a serious problem where there are older members of the family or a permanent invalid.

Another drawback to the 2-story house is the cost of maintenance and up-keep. There is more painting to be done on ladders in the 2-story house, more hard-to-reach windows to wash, etc. But the feeling of security gained from sleeping "upstairs," the ease of heating due to its compactness and the added space dimensions of the house all make this one of the most popular styles of home on the market today.

Retirement Homes

Any of the above houses can be turned into a comfortable retirement house. There are even retired people who live on the first floor of a 2-story house, reserving the second floor as guest rooms for when the out-of-town children come to visit. The upstairs rooms in the one and a half story house can easily be closed off when not needed.

But if you are building a retirement house, the chances are you will want to eliminate those steps. You are probably looking for compact, easy-to-clean rooms adapted to the simpler requirements of one or two people. At the most, you want the few steps of the split foyer. Ideally, you may want to eliminate all steps.

Here again, in choosing your plans, keep your own personal needs in mind. Do include space for a workroom for hobbies such as woodworking or sewing.

This may only be one wall of a carefully planned all-purpose room or it may be a room off to itself. The retirement house is still a dream house—as important to you as the first house you buy—and your planning must be equally as careful and tailored to your family needs.

Vacation Homes

Vacation homes should be planned with the same care as any other. If the vacation house is a second home—the retreat kind of place where the family can escape the world—it is still an investment in more than just money. The happiness of your hideaway can depend on the way it is built and the comfort it offers you.

Here, there is even more reason to be sure that the house fits into its surrounding area. You would not want high, small windows in the mountains to shut out the views you came to see. Likewise, perishable white carpeting would be out of place as well as impractical at the sandy beach. Whether your house is in the country by the lake, in the mountains or at the seashore, be sure it is adaptable to the climatic conditions there. And consider how you are going to use this retreat. Will you be going there for weekends throughout the year? If so, you will have to allow for the elements—the heat in summer and the cold in winter.

Be prepared in your vacation retreat for all kinds of emergencies. Have storage place for what you may need in the event of a sudden power failure, floods or even snow-storms. More than anywhere else, you need to be a Boy or Girl Scout in your vacation home and Be Prepared. For this house, to be successful, must be planned with all the factors in mind—from your own needs and desires to a practical, affordable house in the setting of your choice.

HOUSE

PLANS

Henerdon

Five levels of practical, useful and wasteless living space are found in this attractive split level home. Four large bedrooms are located on the upper levels. The top level bedroom will accommodate two children or it could be left unfinished. Plenty of closets, bathrooms and storage areas are strategically located throughout the house. No. 9219.

AREA	SQ. FT.
Main living levels	—1,369
Top level	— 311
Family room-garage level	— 924
Basement	— 615

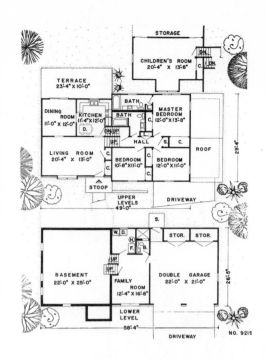

Akron

Entrance foyer sunny, impressive

Sunlight sparkles through expanses of glass framing the foyer of this contemporary split level. Coat closet and planter add convenience and atmosphere. Three well-proportioned bedrooms fill the sleeping area, including a double-closeted master bedroom with private bath and towel closet. Below the bedroom level, garage and storage area border a den, laundry/utility room, and half bath. No. 320.

AREA	SQ. FT.
Upper levels	—1,274
Garage level	— 626
Basement	— 607

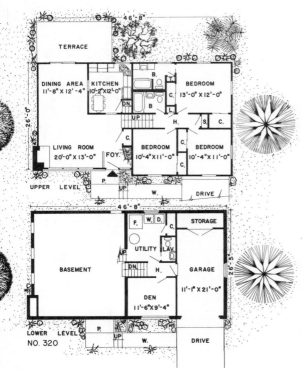

Akron **39**

Wanchester

First floor bedroom sets pace for plan

With double closets, divided bath, and maximum uninterrupted wall space for arranging furniture, the first floor master bedroom typifies this effective plan. Closets, hall, and bath buffer noise and insure privacy, and the bedroom is tucked behind the living room for added quiet. Living and dining room flank the gracious foyer and a hallway leads to informal areas. Equipped with fireplace, the family room includes a breakfast room with bay windowed view of patio, and the kitchen opens to a screened porch. No. 1058.

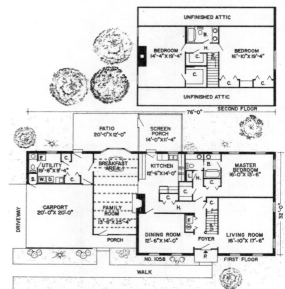

AREA	SQ. FT.
First floor	—1,908
Second floor	— 840
Carport	— 400

Leland

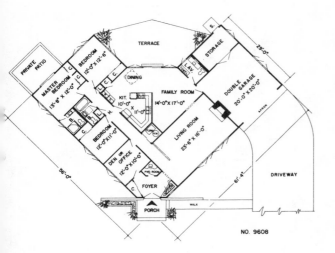

Think big . . .

Here is an unusual looking contemporary design. The attractive entrance foyer contains a large guest closet, planter, powder room and provides access to the den and the living room area. Open planning in the kitchen-family room area provides adequate space for enjoyable family living. This area is well lighted by the overhead clerestory windows. Sliding glass doors at the rear open onto the colorful terrace. The master bedroom features an enclosed private patio which is entered through sliding glass doors. The house may be placed on the lot as shown or placed parallel with the street. No. 9608.

AREA	SQ. FT.
First floor	—2,071
Garage	— 412
Storage	— 112

Trenton

Sophisticated split-level

This strikingly beautiful split level home has a very distinctive exterior. The face brick and battened Redwood siding blend well together with the textured Cedar shakes on the roof. The floor plan is well arranged with three bedrooms, two full baths and plenty of closets on the upper level. The lower level has a large family room with fireplace, a den, bath and storage room. The double garage has a large room behind it which can be used for a workshop, radio shack, hobby room or storage area. No. 9266.

AREA	SQ. FT.
Upper level	—1,661
Lower level	— 782
Garage	— 600

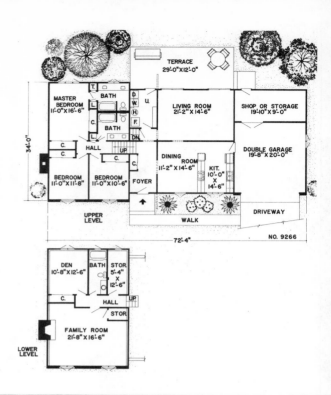

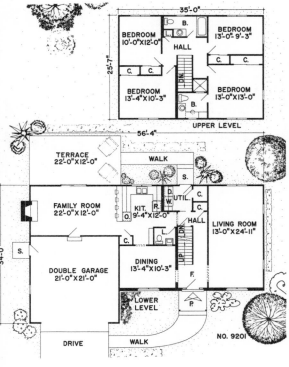

Hedgeston

Increasing land costs are making it necessary to reduce lot sizes and rising building costs demand the strictest building economy. This Traditional two-story home was designed to help meet these problems. Every square foot of area has been used to the best advantage. Four bedrooms and two full baths are located on the second floor. The family room features a wood burning fireplace, and opens onto the terrace through sliding glass doors. No. 9201.

AREA	SQ. FT.
First floor	—1,181
Second floor	— 896
Basement	—1,181
Garage	— 456

Stoneybrook

The deeply raked mortar joints on the stone veneer produce a very textured exterior surface, quite pleasing to the eye. This, plus the stained vertical Red Cedar siding and white trim blend together to form a beautiful home. The interior is very attractive and quite practical, containing three bedrooms, plus a den, living room, family room, kitchen and separate dining room. The screened porch and terrace provide additional living space. No. 9225.

AREA	SQ. FT.
First floor	—2,147
Garage	— 466
Screened porch	— 170

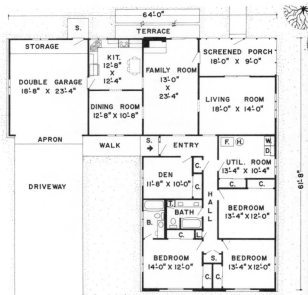

Aries

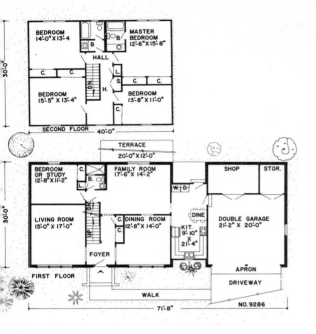

SECOND FLOOR

FIRST FLOOR

It is common knowledge that a two story house provides the maximum amount of living space for the least amount of money. This one features five bedrooms and three full baths. There is a formal dining room and a spacious family room. The large kitchen has an abundance of cabinets, built in an efficient "U" shape. There is also eating space and a laundry area. The garage is 30 feet deep and contains a shop and storage room. This space will house a boat up to 20 ft. long, if the garage partitions are omitted. No. 9286.

AREA	SQ. FT.
First floor	—1,416
Second floor	—1,200
Basement	—1,200
Garage	— 674

Suntown

Contemporary Adds Family Room, Garage

Generously proportioned rooms and cathedral ceilings create an airy feeling in this contemporary expansion plan. A sunken family room with sliding glass doors to terrace, plus a double garage with storage may be completed later. The basic design shows three bedrooms, two full baths, and a kitchen complex with snack bar, dining area, and utility room. No. 334.

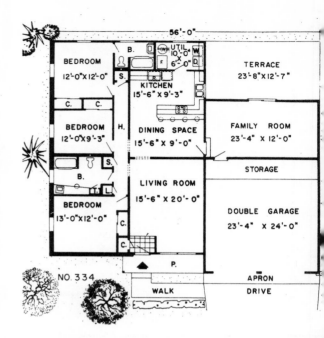

AREA	SQ. FT.
Living area	—1,486
Family room	— 301
Garage	— 583

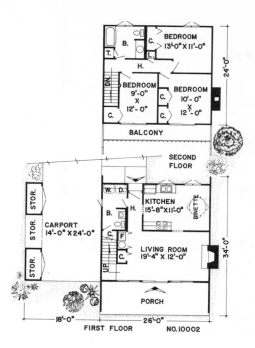

BEDROOM 13'-0" X 11'-0"

BEDROOM 9'-0" X 12'-0"

BEDROOM 10'-0" X 12'-0"

BALCONY

SECOND FLOOR

24'-0"

W. D.

KITCHEN 15'-8" X 11'-0"

DINETTE

CARPORT 14'-0" X 24'-0"

STOR. STOR. STOR. STOR.

LIVING ROOM 19'-4" X 12'-0"

34'-0"

PORCH

18'-0"   26'-0"

FIRST FLOOR   NO. 10002

Highland

Two bedrooms enjoy view, balcony

Two of the three bedrooms in this home open into the redwood balcony via sliding glass doors and share a potentially lovely view. Another bedroom, a large bath with towel closet, and a hall linen closet complete the upper floor. On the main level, the living room, favored with a wood-burning fireplace, borders the roomy kitchen which incorporates an informal dining area. A utility room, bath, and substantial closet space are also supplied on this level. No. 10002.

AREA	SQ. FT.
First floor	—624
Second floor	—624
Carport and storage	—432

Leander

Living room enjoys commanding view

Lounging around the living room's circular fireplace, you will delight in the panorama visible through the three pairs of sliding glass doors. Extending outward is a partially roofed redwood deck doubling as an outdoor living and dining area. Two bedrooms and compartmented bath with shower make up the sleeping area. A well-designed kitchen is furnished with a pass-through to the sizable living room. The garage leaves the option of having its door in front or back, depending on your lot. No. 10024.

AREA	SQ. FT.
First floor	—960
Garage	—288

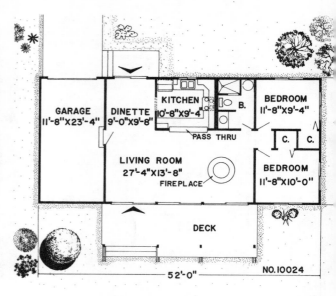

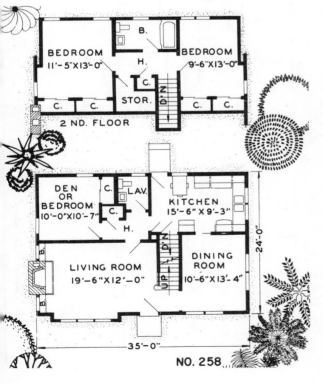

BEDROOM
11'-5"X13'-0"

BEDROOM
9'-6"X13'-0"

B.

H.

C.

C. C. STOR. C. C.

2 ND. FLOOR

DEN
OR
BEDROOM
10'-0"X10'-7"

C. LAV.

C.

H.

KITCHEN
15'-6" X 9'-3"

LIVING ROOM
19'-6"X12'-0"

DINING
ROOM
10'-6"X13'-4"

24'-0"

35'-0"

NO. 258

Haddington

Shake shingles layer rustic traditional

Shuttered dormer windows and brick chimney augment the rustic shake shingles in welding a singular exterior for this two-story traditional. Inside, rooms are fairly sizable and storage space abundant. Living room is placed to the left of the entry and enjoys a fireplace, while dining room borders the kitchen on the right. Two bedrooms upstairs supplement the small bedroom or den with half bath on main level. A spacious full bath is featured upstairs, and double closets furnish each bedroom. No. 258.

AREA	SQ. FT.
First floor	—852
Second floor	—570
Basement	—852

Fairfield

This two story Monterey style family home is quite suitable for a city lot or a suburban tract. This home will retain its value throughout the years. First floor construction is brick veneer. Wood siding is used on the second story. A very desirable floor plan features four bedrooms, a first floor study, three baths and plenty of closets and storage space. The large garage has a shop which can be used for storing a boat if the partition is omitted. The family room has a wood burning fireplace. No. 9272.

AREA	SQ. FT.
First floor	—1,232
Second floor	—1,351
Garage and shop	— 772

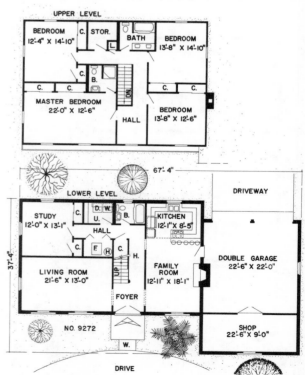

UPPER LEVEL

BEDROOM 12'-4" X 14'-10"   C. STOR.   BATH   BEDROOM 13'-8" X 14'-10"

MASTER BEDROOM 22'-0" X 12'-6"

HALL

BEDROOM 13'-8" X 12'-6"

LOWER LEVEL

67'-4"

DRIVEWAY

STUDY 12'-0" X 13'-1"

HALL

KITCHEN 12'-1" X 8'-5"

37'-4"

DOUBLE GARAGE 22'-6" X 22'-0"

LIVING ROOM 21'-6" X 13'-0"

UP

FAMILY ROOM 12'-11" X 18'-1"

FOYER

NO. 9272

SHOP 22'-6" X 9'-0"

W.

DRIVE

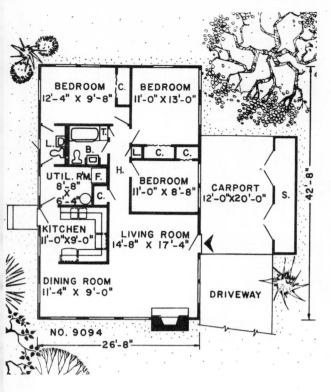

NO. 9094

BEDROOM
12'-4" X 9'-8"

BEDROOM
11'-0" X 13'-0"

UTIL. RM.
8'-8"
X
6'-4"

KITCHEN
11'-0"X9'-0"

BEDROOM
11'-0" X 8'-8"

CARPORT
12'-0"X20'-0"

LIVING ROOM
14'-8" X 17'-4"

DINING ROOM
11'-4" X 9'-0"

DRIVEWAY

42'-8"

26'-8"

Sherrill

Fireplace, cathedral ceilings set mood

Brightened by cathedral ceilings and a wood-burning fireplace, the living and dining room maintains its place as the focus of this comfortable two bedroom home. The bedrooms share a full bath with towel closet, but the half bath may be entered from the left rear bedroom or the utility room, and it is only a few steps from the kitchen. Storage space frames the carport area, and the utility room is large enough to house a customized laundry area with built-in table and shelves. No. 9094.

AREA	SQ. FT.
First floor	—1,140
Carport and storage	— 320

Dawnview

Breakfast bar sets off dining area

Devised for vacation living, this Chalet beach home features several worksaving ideas, including a breakfast bar which divides living room and kitchen. The ample living-dining room spills out onto the attractive 24-foot deck. Four closeted bedrooms include two upstairs, favored with balconies and reached by a spiral staircase off the living room. The home is built on treated pilings but might also be constructed on a conventional foundation. No. 10054.

AREA	SQ. FT.
First floor	—768
Second floor	—406

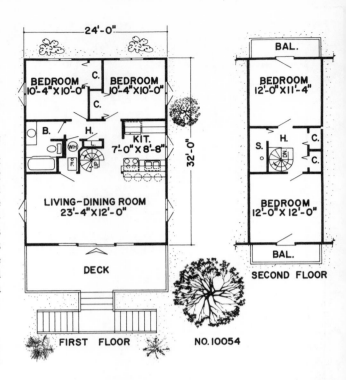

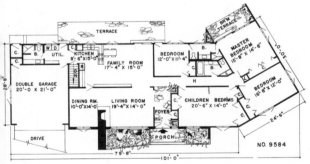

Irvingham

Zoned for work, play and sleep . . .

This five-bedroom ranch design is a practical solution to the housing problem of growing modern families who prefer a one-level house. It is zoned to separate varying activities of family life, yet has easy interrelationship. The open kitchen is arranged to provide easy access to the laundry, dining and family areas while still having ample floor space for all kitchen activities. The large children's bedroom can be used as a play area in the daytime and then separated at night with a folding partition. The master bedroom has its own private terrace which is screened on the outside with a stone wall. A partial basement is provided for heating equipment, storage, etc. No. 9584.

AREA	SQ. FT.
First floor	—2,300
Basement	— 900
Garage	— 432

Mardale

Plan boasts accommodating kitchen

Handy to patio, family room and living room, the kitchen in this home offers a snack bar and a garage entrance. Convenience marks the entire plan, which supplies a closeted entrance foyer to channel traffic. Warm and cozy, the family room is furnished with wood-burning fireplace. Three ample bedrooms share two full baths. No. 1008.

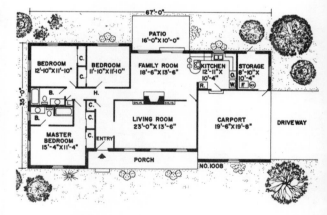

AREA	SQ. FT.
First floor	—1,510
Storage room	— 108
Carport	— 417

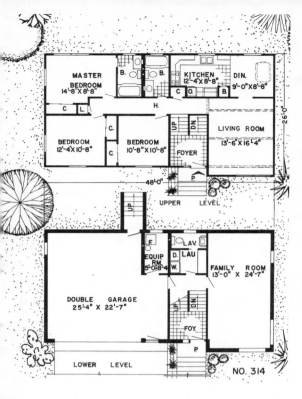

MASTER BEDROOM
14'-8" X 8'-8"

B.

KITCHEN
12'-4" X 8'-8"

DIN.
9'-0" X 8'-8"

C. O.

B.

C.

L.

H.

BEDROOM
12'-4" X 10'-8"

BEDROOM
10'-8" X 10'-8"

C.

UP DN

FOYER

LIVING ROOM
13'-6" X 16'-4"

26'-0"

48'-0"

UPPER LEVEL

UP

E.

EQUIP RM
5'-0" X 8'-4"

LAV.

D. LAU
W.

FAMILY ROOM
13'-0" X 24'-7"

DOUBLE GARAGE
25'-4" X 22'-7"

UP DN

FOY.

P.

LOWER LEVEL

NO. 314

Craigmoor

Equipment room completes lower level

Housing a huge family room, laundry center and half bath, the lower level of this split foyer plan also outlines an equipment room that fringes the extra large double garage. Upstairs, the living room boasts exposed beams and the dining area is open to the sizable tiled kitchen. Back-to-back baths, one private to the master bedroom, serve the zoned bedroom wing, and two hall closets are outlined. Garage features two outside entrances. No. 314.

AREA	SQ. FT.
Upper level	—1,180
Lower level	—1,180

San Miguel

Design Boasts Spanish Accent . . .

Grillwork and graceful arches add a touch of Spain to the impressive brick-sheathed exterior of this three bedroom home. Inside, the plan outlines a central hallway radiating from the foyer and allowing ready access to every room. Formal living room enjoys a restful wood-burning fireplace. No. 10146.

AREA	SQ. FT.
First floor	—1,498
Basement	—1,498
Garage	— 576

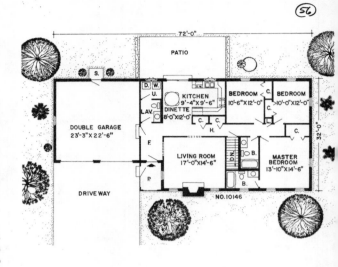

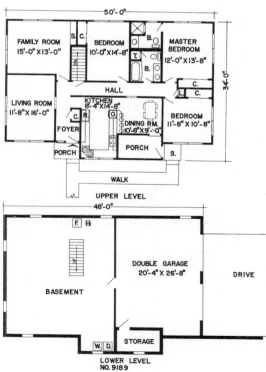

FAMILY ROOM
15'-0" X 13'-0"

BEDROOM
10'-0" X14'-8"

MASTER
BEDROOM
12'-0" X 13'-8"

HALL

LIVING ROOM
11'-8" X 16'-0"

KITCHEN
8'-4" X 14'-8"

DINING RM.
10'-8" X 9'-0"

BEDROOM
11'-8" X 10'-8"

FOYER

PORCH

PORCH

WALK

UPPER LEVEL

50'-0"

34'-0"

48'-0"

BASEMENT

DOUBLE GARAGE
20'-4" X 26'-8"

DRIVE

STORAGE

W. D.

LOWER LEVEL
NO. 9189

Woodson

This design utilizes a sloping lot by housing the garage in the basement. This assures easy car starting every morning and provides a comfortable place for a workshop. A boat building enthusiast will really appreciate the convenience. The floor plan was designed with the housewife in mind. The kitchen is the nucleus of the home and is located only a few steps from every room in the house. This will save the busy housewife many steps in the management of the home. A very efficient floor plan is provided. No. 9189.

AREA	SQ. FT.
First floor	—1,516
Basement	—1,001
Garage	— 519
Porch	— 64

Woodson 57

Hermanas

Overhead beams dominate entrance

Towering diamond light windows, and stone arches shape the facade of this Mediterranean design, intensified by massive beams overhanging the entrance. Height is emphasized in this plan, continuing with cathedral ceilings that top the sunken living room. Paneled and cheered by a wood-burning fireplace, the family room extends the width of the home and opens to rear terrace. Nestled in the sleeping wing are three sizable bedrooms, including master bedroom with walk-in closet, dressing area, and segmented bath as well as sliding glass doors to the terrace. No. 10000.

AREA	SQ. FT.
First floor	—2,103
Basement	—1,807
Garage	— 569

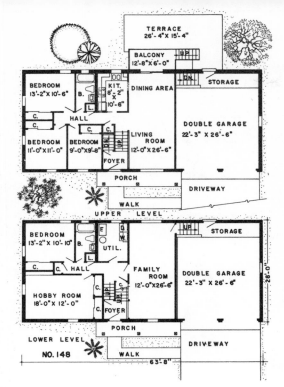

Melville

Ever popular Colonial styling has been used on this attractive split foyer design. The Old English brick, white louvered shutters and the tall wooden columns provide dignity to the exterior. There are three bedrooms shown on the lower level. Each room has a closet of above average size. The living-dining room is quite large and can utilize a scenic view from both ends. The lower level contains recreational areas, providing both family room and hobby room. The hobby room can also serve as an extra bedroom or guest room. The garage is extra large and provides storage space at the rear as well as access to the family room. No. 148.

AREA	SQ. FT.
Upper level	—1,140
Lower level	—1,140
Garage	— 644

Laughton

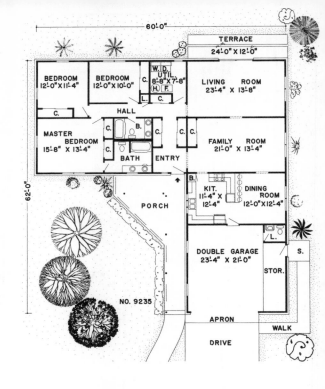

The colors of the roof, the battened siding and the brick definitely complement each other. This produces an exterior facade which is very pleasing to the eye. The covered front porch provides a shady place to sit and enjoy the outdoors. In addition to its exterior appeal, it has a fine floor plan. The rooms are large and there is an abundance of closets. The lavatory in the garage will be appreciated by the man of the house. No. 9235.

AREA	SQ. FT.
First floor	—2,056
Garage	— 541

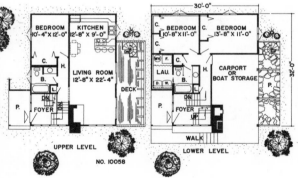

UPPER LEVEL

LOWER LEVEL

NO. 10058

BEDROOM 10'-4" X 12'-0"

KITCHEN 12'-8" X 9'-0"

LIVING ROOM 12'-8" X 22'-4"

DECK

FOYER

30'-0"

32'-0"

BEDROOM 10'-8" X 11'-0"

BEDROOM 13'-8" X 11'-0"

LAU.

CARPORT OR BOAT STORAGE

FOYER UP

WALK

Highpoint

Elevated sun deck savors scenery

High enough to capture a sweeping view, the wooden deck joins the sliding glass doors in permeating the living room with light and scenery. The open living, dining and kitchen area boasts a fireplace and breakfast bar. Besides the bedroom and bath on the upper level, two more bedrooms, a bath, and a laundry room comprise the lower level. Housed in the fireplace foundation in the carport is a built-in barbecue, serviceable in any weather. No. 10058.

AREA	SQ. FT.
Lower level	— 636
Upper level	— 768
Carport	— 264

Isley

Five bedrooms plus a den are designed into this beautiful contemporary split level home. The floor plan is perfect. The foyer channels traffic to all areas of the house, preserving privacy for each room. All of the bedrooms have at least eight feet of closet space and the master bedroom has two six-foot closets. There are two full baths on the upper level and a bath with shower on the lower level. The garage is extra large and has an abundance of storage space. The recreation room will serve as the family room and will probably be the most popular room in the house. No. 9251.

AREA	SQ. FT.
Upper levels	—2,118
Lower level	—1,250
Garage and storage	— 889

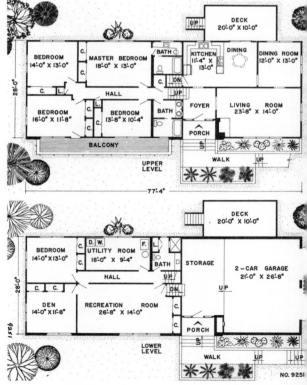

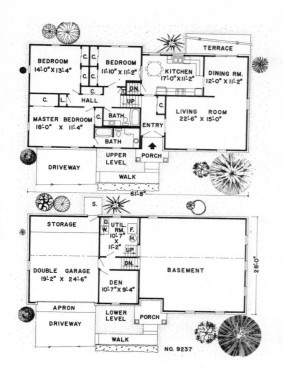

Balsam

The massive front entrance of this beautiful split level home possesses a stately appearance which is very impressive. A very desirable floor plan arrangement provides excellent circulation throughout the house. Each bedroom has two large closets. Sliding glass doors in the dining room open onto the terrace at the rear. The large basement can be finished into an attractive recreation room. No. 9237.

AREA	SQ. FT.
Living areas	—1,748
Garage, den and utility	— 822
Basement	— 820

Terrymoor

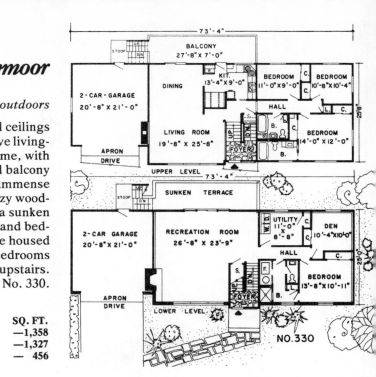

Balcony draws dining outdoors

Expanses of windows and cathedral ceilings create light and space in the extensive living-dining area of this split foyer home, with dining area opening to outdoors and balcony via sliding glass doors. Beneath, an immense recreation room is favored with cozy wood-burning fireplace and opens to a sunken terrace. Utility room, closeted den and bedroom, and full bath with shower are housed on this level, while another three bedrooms and two full baths are provided upstairs. No. 330.

AREA	SQ. FT.
Upper level	—1,358
Lower level	—1,327
Garage	— 456

Oakwood

Traditional design; modern features

Two stories plus a full unfinished basement provide over 3,000 square feet of usable living space in this attractive home. The master bedroom of this traditional home boasts two large closets, a built in vanity and a private bath. Notice that the linen closet is accessible from two sides. No. 370.

AREA	SQ. FT.
First floor	—1,008
Second floor	—1,008
Basement	—1,008
Garage	— 570

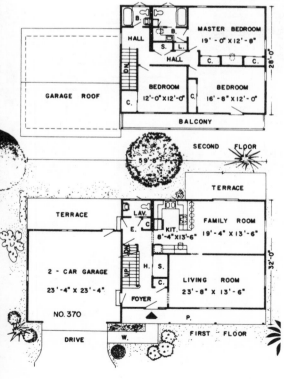

Kellam

Secluded patio, garden and terrace

This house is completely contemporary and offers easy living for the entire family. The master bedroom has access to the covered terrace and also has its own private bath with tiled shower. Sliding glass doors open onto the terrace from the living room. The kitchen and family room open onto a small flagstone patio which serves as an outdoor dining area. The enclosed garden across the front of the house is an unusual but desirable feature. The portico (walkway covering) is both functional and attractive. It helps form a secluded garden retreat and also serves as a covered walkway from the garage to the main entrance. No. 9586.

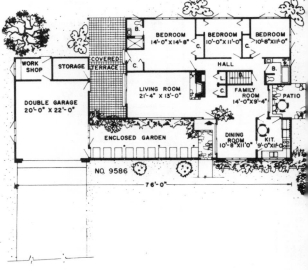

AREA	SQ. FT.
First floor	—1,490
Basement	—1,245
Garage	— 609

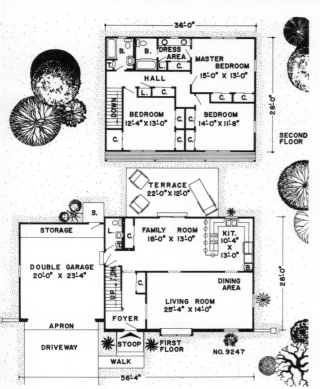

Fallbrook

This house has all the lovely features that can make family life so pleasant. It has an impressive entrance foyer, an extra large living room, family room, kitchen and lavatory on the first floor. The second floor features three large bedrooms, two full baths, eight clothes closets, two linen closets and a towel closet. For a family on a moderate building budget, this two-story house will be hard to beat. No. 9247.

AREA	SQ. FT.
First floor	—1,022
Second floor	—1,008
Basement	—1,022
Garage	— 495

Dallas

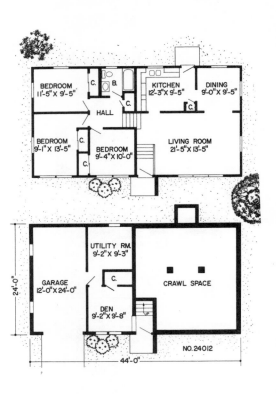

Split level stresses convenience

With living areas set on three separate levels, this design displays a floor plan that focuses on the main living level and puts all other areas within easy reach. The main level, up from the foyer, incorporates an airy living room, formal dining room, and large kitchen. Up a few steps is the quiet sleeping section, composed of three bedrooms and a sizable bath with linen closet. Below, a closeted den can double as extra sleeping space if needed. No. 24012.

AREA	SQ. FT.
Living area	—1,056
Garage, den and utility	— 528

Graymoor

Colonial-past and present . . .

The graceful, columned porch of this house recalls the style of old Southern mansions. This, blended with the white siding and dark shutters produce a very attractive home. The split foyer floor plan utilizes every square foot of space without waste. Sliding glass doors in the large living room open onto a wood deck at the rear. The two large closets in the garage provide plenty of storage space. This house will fit nicely on a 60-foot lot. No. 9278.

AREA	SQ. FT.
Upper level	—1,144
Family room	— 632
Garage	— 512

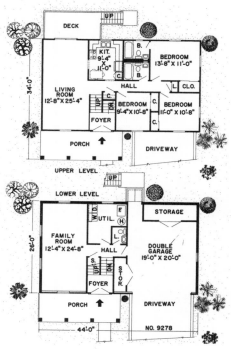

Edgarton

Charm, practicality blend in plan

Imposing columns and shuttered small-paned windows paint a picturesque facade for this three bedroom traditional. Inside and out, the plan fuses charm with convenience to produce covered patio, tiled foyer, and cozy family room. No. 1006.

AREA	SQ. FT.
First floor	—1,300
Carport	— 400
Exterior storage	— 60

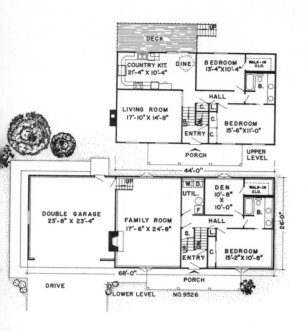

Faxon

Country kitchen dines on elevated deck

Colonial charm apparent on the exterior of this rectangular split foyer plan is carried inside and exuded in the huge country kitchen with sliding glass doors to elevated wooden deck. Formal and isolated living room supplements cozy family room with wood-burning fireplace. Three closeted bedrooms share two full baths, each with double sinks, and lower level den with excellent walk-in closet might be relied on for sleeping quarters. Laundry-utility room borders the family room. No. 9326.

AREA	SQ. FT.
Upper level	—1,144
Lower level	—1,144
Garage	— 576

Richland

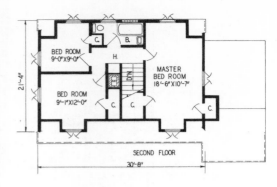

SECOND FLOOR

All of the dignity and charm of the traditional Colonial home has been combined with an excellent floor plan to produce this modification of the basic Cape Cod plan. If the garage is omitted the house will have a frontage of only 31 ft. making it suitable for a narrow city lot. No. 5035.

AREA	SQ. FT.
First floor	—726
Second floor	—622
Basement	—726

FIRST FLOOR

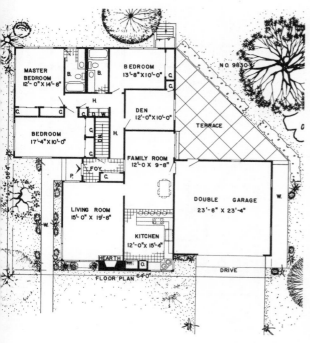

Quincy

Country Kitchen Boasts Barbecue Grill

Quaint and colorful, the country kitchen of this hipped-roof home is favored with a built-in barbecue and a breakfast bar that separates it from the family room. Carefully detailed, the plan assigns the family room sliding glass doors to take advantage of the triangular terrace and the well-windowed living room a pleasurable wood-burning fireplace. Bedrooms are placed to the rear of the design and include a nicely-proportioned master bedroom with bath, two more substantial bedrooms, and a slightly smaller den. No. 9830.

AREA	SQ. FT.
First floor	—1,782
Basement	—1,782
Garage	— 576

Empress

Well-arranged kitchen bonus in plan

Favored with a convenient pantry, breakfast area, and plentiful closet space, the carefully designed kitchen is only one of the attractions in this split foyer plan. The living room's fireplace is enjoyed in the dining area as well, and another fireplace brightens the elongated family room. Three bedrooms include a cozy master bedroom with private bath, and two hall linen closets are proposed. A laundry and utility room on the lower level also includes a half-bath. No. 9042.

AREA	SQ. FT.
Upper level	—1,302
Lower level	— 687
Garage and storage	— 561

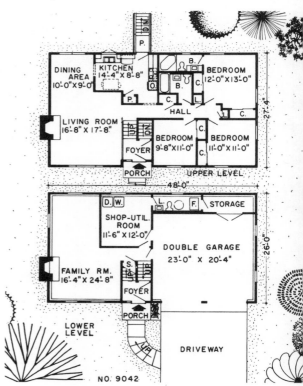

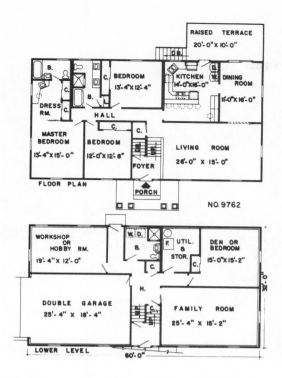

RAISED TERRACE
20'-0" X 10'-0"

BEDROOM
13'-4" X 12'-4"

KITCHEN
14'-0" X 16'-0"

DINING ROOM
11'-0" X 16'-0"

B.

DRESS RM.

HALL

MASTER BEDROOM
13'-4" X 15'-0"

BEDROOM
12'-0" X 12'-8"

FOYER

LIVING ROOM
26'-0" X 15'-0"

FLOOR PLAN

PORCH

NO. 9762

WORKSHOP OR HOBBY RM.
19'-4" X 12'-0"

W.D.

UTIL. & STOR.

DEN OR BEDROOM
15'-0" X 15'-2"

DOUBLE GARAGE
25'-4" X 18'-4"

FAMILY ROOM
25'-4" X 15'-2"

LOWER LEVEL

60'-0"

Viceroy

Contemporary convenience fills colonial

Handsome white columns mark the entrance to this delightful Colonial, which harmonizes a traditional facade with an up-to-date interior. The split foyer arrangement itself is a practical choice which permits easy access to the sprawling family room and hobby shop below. Upstairs, the master bedroom profits by the extensive bath and dressing area, and the carefully calculated kitchen chooses a breakfast bar, planning desk, and copious cabinet space. The separate dining room spills out to a raised terrace via sliding glass doors. No. 9762.

AREA	SQ. FT.
First floor	—1,832
Basement	—1,519
Garage	— 504

Cheyenne

Redwood Bridge Fronts Contemporary . . .

Leading to double entrance doors and a lavish foyer, a redwood bridge expresses the unique, natural flavor of this three bedroom contemporary. Immediately visible from the foyer is the fireplace lighting the expansive sunken living room. Redwood deck beyond is accessible through two pairs of sliding glass doors. No. 10148.

AREA	SQ. FT.
First floor	—2,050
Basement	—2,050
Garage	— 440

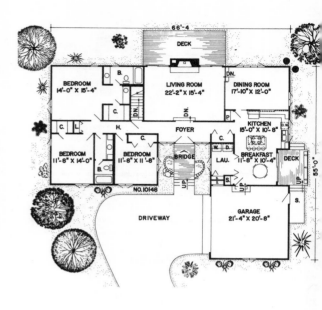

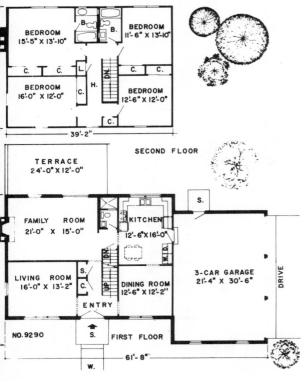

BEDROOM
15'-5" X 13'-10"

BEDROOM
11'-6" X 13'-10"

BEDROOM
16'-0" X 12'-0"

BEDROOM
12'-6" X 12'-0"

39'-2"

SECOND FLOOR

TERRACE
24'-0" X 12'-0"

FAMILY ROOM
21'-0" X 15'-0"

KITCHEN
12'-6" X 16'-0"

LIVING ROOM
16'-0" X 13'-2"

DINING ROOM
12'-6" X 12'-2"

3-CAR GARAGE
21'-4" X 30'-6"

DRIVE

ENTRY

NO. 9290

FIRST FLOOR

61'-8"

W.

Girard

French Provincial styling, a low maintain-
ence exterior and an excellent floor plan are
combined to produce this very desirable
family home. The exterior is brick veneer
and cedar shingles, a very harmonious combination. Four bedrooms, two full baths
and seven closets are located on the second
floor. A bath with shower is found on the
first floor and is convenient to both the
kitchen and family room. Wood burning
fireplaces are located in the family room and
basement. A three car garage provides
space for the family boat. No. 9290.

AREA	SQ. FT.
First floor	—1,190
Second floor	—1,145
Basement	—1,200
Garage	— 708

Townsite

Multi-level shaped for sloping site

Tailored to a sloping lot, this multi-level design encases three generous bedrooms and three full baths within its brick-layered exterior. Zoning the top level for sleep insures maximum quiet. Living areas are accessible directly from the entry and include a large living room, glowing with wood-burning fireplace, a formal dining room and kitchen with ample counter space and eating area. Below the sleeping level is a sizable den bordered by full bath and useful as an extra bedroom. No. 178.

AREA	SQ. FT.
Living area	—1,861
Garage level	— 914
Basement level	— 921

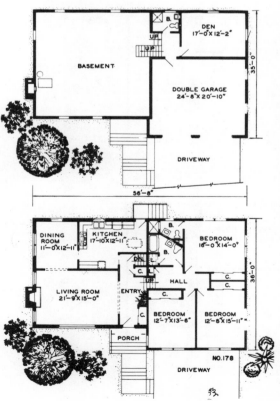

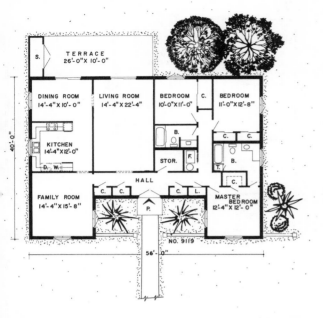

Warner

This beautiful white brick, French Provincial design will retain its dignity and resale value as long as it stands. The brick and cedar shingled, hip roof assures a low maintance exterior. A well designed and very efficient floor plan will provide comfortable family living. The house is basementless, therefore, an abundance of storage space is provided. Both the living room and the dining room have sliding glass doors which open onto the terrace at the rear. No. 9119.

AREA	SQ. FT.
First floor	—1,980

Barbary

Leisure plan poised for outdoor fun

Encircled by wood decks and walkways, this two bedroom vacation home opens to the outdoors on three sides for maximum enjoyment of its surroundings. Two sizable bedrooms, each favored with two closets, are separated by a compartmented bath, with the bordering laundry niche a welcome addition. Kitchen, living and dining rooms form an open area for meals and entertaining that merits an indoor barbecue grill and wood-burning fireplace. A full bath with shower is well-placed next to the deck entrance. No. 10194.

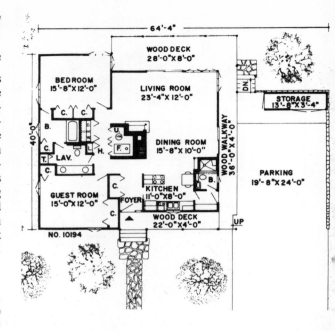

AREA	SQ. FT.
First floor	—1,418
Parking	— 480
Outdoor storage	— 56

Laurel

Tri-level plan livable year round

Set to savor the scenery from four sides and three levels, this three bedroom plan does double duty as a leisure design and a home for year round living. A patio extends the basement level, while decks edge and encircle the first and second floors. For efficiency, the kitchen is large and shows built-in snack bar and deck entry. Closet space is plentiful in bedrooms and hallways, and three full compartmented baths are featured. No. 10222.

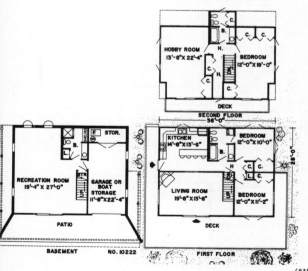

AREA	SQ. FT.
First floor	—1,008
Second floor	— 851
Basement	—1,008

Osborn

Exposed stone wall accents living room

Set apart from the main body of the home, the living room in this plan is highlighted by an array of windows and a natural stone wall. Adjoining the living room is a formal dining room and beyond that is a highly efficient kitchen endowed with built-in dishwasher, desk, snack bar, and space for washer, dryer, and large broom closet. The informal family room opens through sliding glass doors to the terrace and houses an open stairway to the basement. Three bedrooms and two and a half baths are specified. No. 9778.

AREA	SQ. FT.
First floor	—2,060
Basement	—2,060
Garage	— 484

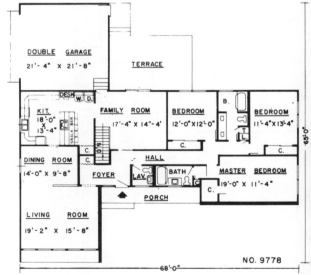

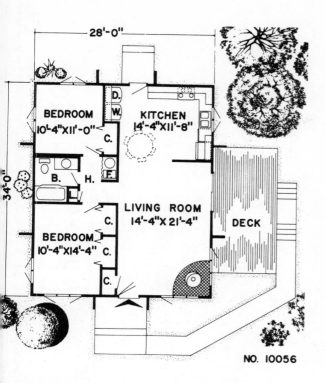

NO. 10056

Beachside

Sizable kitchen accents compact design

Kitchen and living room area in this all-season home comprise over half the home and encourages relaxed comfort, whether this is to be used as a vacation retreat or permanent residence. The kitchen houses a dining area and space for a washer and dryer, certainly a convenience. Two large bedrooms utilize a great deal of closet space and a hall linen closet and living room closet provide additional space. A corner fireplace and access to the wooden deck further complement the living room. No. 10056.

AREA	SQ. FT.
Main floor	—952
Deck	—200

Belleview

Leaded glass doors gild authentic plan

Leaded glass doors, brick arches, and a traditional chimney are among the authentic French Provincial touches in this extensive four bedroom design. Styled for relaxed living, the family room opens to a wooden deck, while the living and dining rooms open to the terrace and pool area. The master bedroom appendages a separate sitting room as well as a bath and two closets. Two more baths, including one near the pool area, serve the three remaining bedrooms. A convenient laundry area adjoins the kitchen. No. 9970.

AREA	SQ. FT.
First floor	—2,814
Basement	—1,358
Garage	— 686

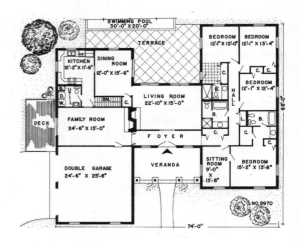

Chateau

Chalet can be finished as needed

Swiss Chalet inspired, this home allows the possibility of using it while completing the attic bedroom or lower bedroom and family room at some later date. The first floor, housing living room, kitchen, full size bedroom and bath and even a laundry would make a more than comfortable retreat until the home could be finished. No. 10026.

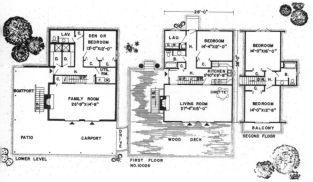

AREA	SQ. FT.
First floor	—1,052
Second floor	— 628
Lower level	—1,052

Utrecht

Novel design focuses on outdoor fun

Centering on life in the open air, this novel exterior appendages not only a balcony, open deck and terrace, but a glassed-in porch that converts to a screened-in porch for summer use. The master bedroom with private bath augments two upstairs bedroom and a den in the basement that could generate a fourth bedroom. Also featured is a thirty foot basement recreation room flanking the terrace, plus a family room opposite the glassed-in porch. No. 9890.

AREA	SQ. FT.
First floor	—1,280
Second floor	— 448
Basement	—1,280

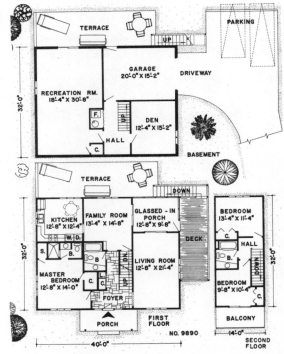

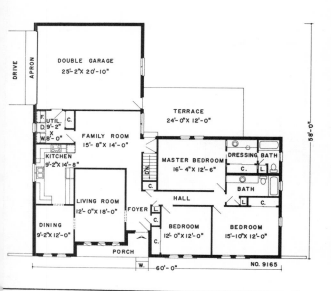

Stoneville

Special attraction: Master bedroom . . .

Just enough natural stone trim has been added to the brick veneer of this beautiful home to create a very attractive and interesting facade. The interior is equally desirable showing a very efficient and practical floor plan. This home has a separate dining room as well as a family room and it has a utility room as well as a basement. The master bedroom has a very nice bath, dressing room, closet area. The extra large second bath serves the other two bedrooms. No. 9165.

AREA	SQ. FT.
First floor	—1,907
Basement	—1,907
Garage	— 577

Parlington

A practical plan throughout . . .

A low maintenance exterior is provided on this home by specifying brick veneer and a cedar shake shingle roof. The hip roof eliminates all gable ends for additional maintenance savings. A very practical floor plan shows three bedrooms, extra large closets and two and one-half baths. The family room, while also serving as the dining room, is large enough for TV viewing and family activities. A full basement provides plenty of space for a large recreation area as well as storage and utility space. No. 9814.

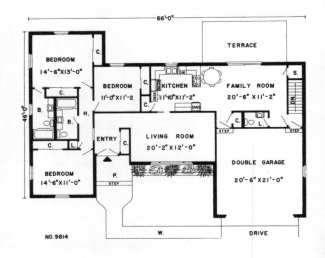

AREA	SQ. FT.
First floor	—1,798
Basement	—1,798
Garage	— 476

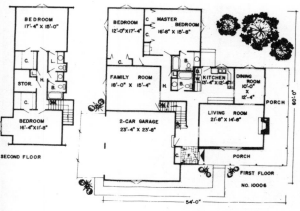

SECOND FLOOR

FIRST FLOOR
NO. 10006

Oakengates

Tudor plan annexes roofed porch

Contrasting stone and stucco slashed with
rough timbers give character to this English
Tudor plan, extended on two sides by a
roofed porch. Rooms are proportioned for
efficiency, especially the second floor bath
complex, segmented to allow maximum use.
Taking command in the living room is a
warm wood-burning fireplace, and the
attached dining room is furnished with
sliding glass doors to the porch area. A
built-in dressing table benefits the master
bedroom, which also includes a full bath and
double closets. No. 10006.

AREA	SQ. FT.
First floor	—1,926
Second floor	— 864
Garage	— 583
Basement	—1,926

LeMans

Sun Deck Open For Sleeping, Recreation

Separating an enormous recreation room and five bedroom sleeping wing, the sun deck efficiently serves all areas of this rustic contemporary. Master bedroom is set apart on the first floor and opens to a private patio Formal living and dining rooms are supplemented by fireplace-brightened family room opening to terrace. Casual dining space is provided in the kitchen, bordered by laundry and half bath. Isolated and zoned for activity, the recreation room is a natural setting for parties, with a minimum amount of noise transmitted to main living areas. No. 9984.

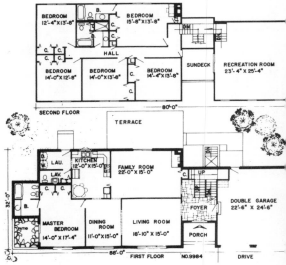

AREA	SQ. FT.
First floor	—1,748
Second floor	—2,096
Basement	—1,652
Garage	— 624

Granger

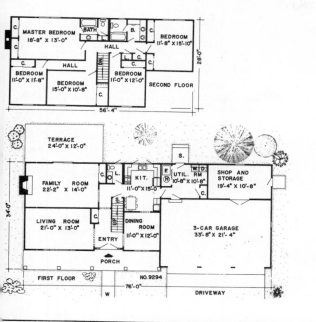

Well designed, two story Southern Colonial designs retain their value and desirability indefinitely. This one has many features which are only found in a custom built home. It has five bedrooms and two full baths on the second floor. The bedroom over the utility room can easily be omitted if not needed. The 3-car garage will provide space for a boat as well as two cars. The first floor rooms are quite spacious and arrange to provide access to each one without crossing through another. The family room has a wood burning fireplace and sliding glass doors which open onto a large terrace. No. 9294.

AREA	SQ. FT.
First floor	—1,329
Second floor	—1,412
Garage and storage	— 961

Falkland

Rustic design blends into hillside

Naturally perfect for a woodland setting, this redwood decked home will adapt equally well to a lake or ocean setting. A car or boat garage is furnished on the lower level. Fireplaces equip both the living room and the 36-foot long family room which opens onto a shaded patio. A laundry room adjoins the open kitchen which shares the large redwood deck encircling the living and dining area. Two bedrooms and two full baths on the first floor supplement another bedroom and half bath on the lower level. No. 10012.

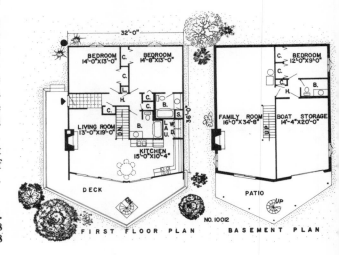

AREA	SQ. FT.
First floor	—1,198
Basement	—1,198

Richmond

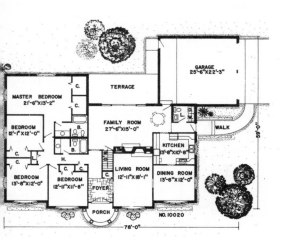

Colonial detailing enlivens exterior

Impressive Colonial columns punctuate the semi-circular porch and fuse with the bow windows and brick to create an exceptional facade. Inside, the floor plan is a study in modern living. Fireplaces grace both living room and family room, which opens to an expansive terrace. A formal dining room adjoins the highly functional kitchen, and the 21 foot master bedroom boasts a lavish full bath and double closets. Two front bedrooms are accented with lovely bow windows. No. 10020.

AREA	SQ. FT.
First floor	—2,512
Basement	—2,512
Garage	— 648

Flambeau

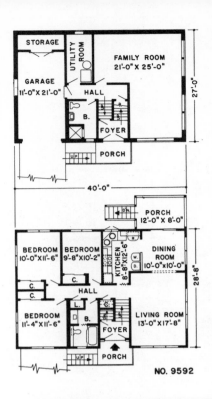

Planned for family comfort . . .

Here's a wonderfully functional plan with much more living space than is usually found in a house which is only forty feet wide. The double entrance doors and mid-level foyer add an air of luxury to the exterior appearance. Two full baths are provided, one on each level. The wood panelled family room is very large and will undoubtedly be the most popular area in the house. The furnace and water heater are centrally located for maximum efficiency and economy of construction. No. 9592.

AREA	SQ. FT.
Living area	—1,148
Family room	— 467
Garage	— 681

NO. 9592

Stovall

Outdoor living awaits summer

Relaxing outdoor barbecues and fun-filled parties will find a natural setting in the inviting outdoor dining room of this bi-level design. Inside, an immense recreation room provides an alternative and is bordered by a den and full bath. Three bedrooms are found on the upper level, including a master bedroom with lavish private bath with shower. The elongated living room features a fireplace and dining area and skirts a sizable kitchen with laundry and eating space. No. 9046.

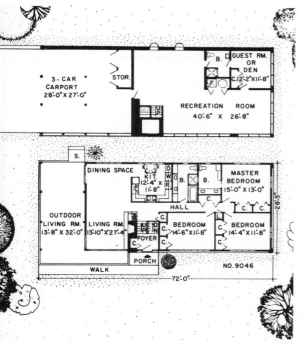

AREA	SQ. FT.
First Floor	—1,624
Basement	—1,130
Carport	— 784

Mandano

Spanish Style Designed To Grow

Essentially a simple layout, this Spanish-flavored ranch style sets either the double garage or two end bedrooms for future completion. Stately arches dramatize the facade, and a final total of three bedrooms and two full baths are shown. The well-proportioned living room is bordered by a kitchen with dining area and access to the patio. No. 10122.

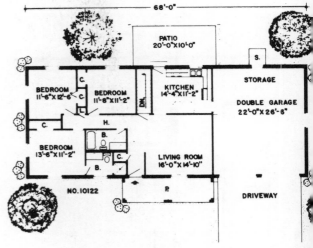

AREA	SQ. FT.
Living area	— 882
End bedrooms	— 392
Garage	— 636

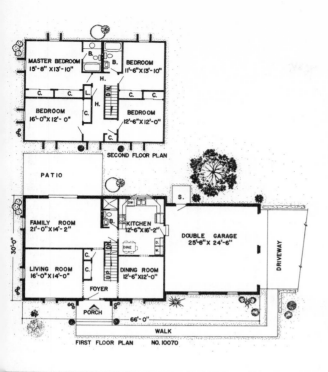

MASTER BEDROOM
15'-8" X 13'-10"

BEDROOM
11'-6" X 13'-10"

BEDROOM
16'-0" X 12'-0"

BEDROOM
12'-6" X 12'-0"

SECOND FLOOR PLAN

PATIO

FAMILY ROOM
21'-0" X 14'-2"

KITCHEN
12'-6" X 16'-2"

DOUBLE GARAGE
25'-6" X 24'-6"

DRIVEWAY

LIVING ROOM
16'-0" X 14'-4"

DINING ROOM
12'-6" X 12'-0"

FOYER

PORCH

66'-0"

30'-0"

WALK

FIRST FLOOR PLAN   NO. 10070

Mandeville

Dignity, Formality permeates design

French Provincial styling is given contemporary treatment in this expansive design, characterized by dignity on the exterior and formality within. Formal living and dining rooms wing the foyer and contrast with casual family room, terrace and kitchen at rear of plan. Kitchen allots dining and laundry areas and borders a full bath with shower. Four sizable bedrooms fill the upstairs, with master bedroom meriting double closets and private bath. No. 10070.

AREA	SQ. FT.
First floor	—1,200
Second floor	—1,145
Basement	—1,200
Garage	— 676

Vendome

Abundance of windows absorbs scenery

Bountiful expanses of glass, outlined in red cedar and underscored with wooden decks, dazzle the interior of this singular home with reflections of the surrounding beauty. Each of the three bedrooms boasts abundant closet space and a balcony, and each level houses a full bath. A wood-burning fireplace lights the living room and adjoining dining area, both of which are equipped with sliding glass doors to the deck. The functional kitchen supplies a breakfast bar fringing the dining room. No. 9962.

AREA	SQ. FT.
First floor	—1,056
Second floor	— 893

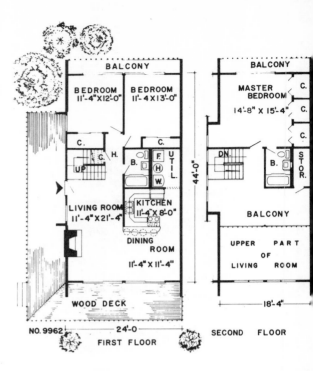

BALCONY

BEDROOM 11'-4" X 12'-0"   BEDROOM 11'-4 X 13'-0"

MASTER BEDROOM 14'-8" X 15'-4"

LIVING ROOM 11'-4" X 21'-4"

KITCHEN 11'-4" X 8'-0"

DINING ROOM 11'-4" X 11'-4"

WOOD DECK

NO. 9962   24'-0   FIRST FLOOR

BALCONY

UPPER PART OF LIVING ROOM

18'-4"   SECOND FLOOR

44'-0"

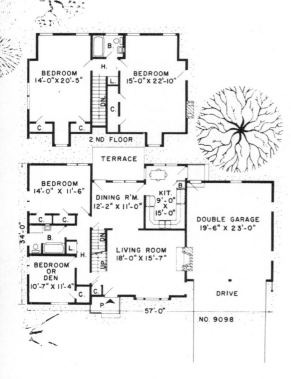

BEDROOM
14'-0" X 20'-5"

BEDROOM
15'-0" X 22'-10"

2 ND FLOOR

TERRACE

BEDROOM
14'-0" X 11'-6"

DINING R'M.
12'-2" X 11'-0"

KIT.
9'-0"
X
15'-0"

DOUBLE GARAGE
19'-6" X 23'-0"

BEDROOM
OR
DEN
10'-7" X 11'-4"

LIVING ROOM
18'-0" X 15'-7"

DRIVE

34'-0"

57'-0"

NO. 9098

Addison

Cape Cod adapts to modern living

Charmingly traditional in appearance, this Cape Cod design incorporates four sizable bedrooms, a compartmented bath, and a terrace, among other features that make it a highly livable plan. The efficient kitchen outlines a breakfast nook overlooking the terrace, and the living room enjoys a fireplace and adjoins the separate dining room. Dormer windows add interest to the upstairs bedrooms, which are spacious and well furnished with closet space. The downstairs bedrooms, one of which may serve as a den, share a compartmented bath. No. 9098.

AREA	SQ. FT.
First floor	—1,142
Second floor	— 900
Garage	— 480
Porch	— 96
Basement	—1,142

Sterling

Built-up Roof Characterizes Cottage

Vertical siding and a chimney clothed in brick fuse with the built-up roof to fashion an exceptional facade for this modest home. The living and dining room is alive with light from the wood-burning fireplace and expanse of windows. Two of the bedrooms share the hall bath, which is also convenient to the kitchen, while the master bedroom enjoys its own half bath. A storage cabinet is allotted off the sizable garage, large enough for a hobby shop or additional storage shelves. No. 184.

AREA	SQ. FT.
First floor	—1,244
Garage	— 290

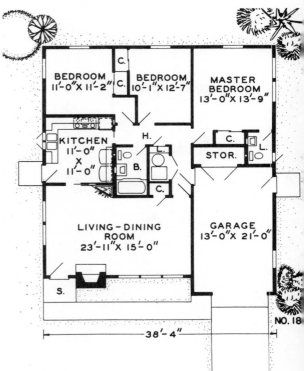

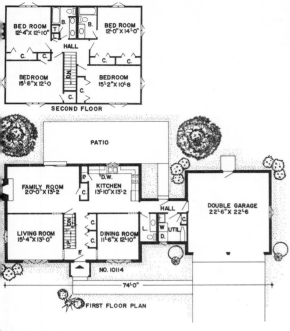

Buckingham

Four Bedrooms for Family Life

English Tudor on the outside and comfort on the inside, this four bedroom home is designed for practical living while remaining simple. Access to the living room and dining room is from both the foyer and the back of the house minimizing everyday traffic without restricting their use for entertainment. Even the fireplace in the family room and the sliding glass door to the patio accent family life. No. 10114.

AREA	SQ. FT.
First floor	—1,220
Second floor	—1,064
Basement	—1,064
Garage	— 576

Holly

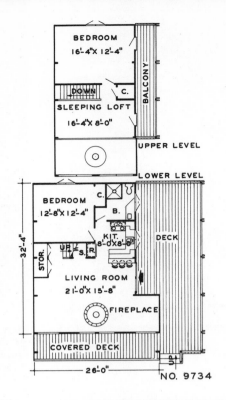

A-Frame enjoys view from all angles

Upper balcony, large wooden deck and expanses of windows in this modified A-frame permit maximum enjoyment of the natural surroundings . . . whether on a wooded hillside or along the seashore. Two large bedrooms, plus a sleeping loft that would easily accommodate bunk beds, translate into a great deal of sleeping space. No. 9734.

AREA	SQ. FT.
Main floor	—727
Upper level	—406

Northwood

Balconies benefit from sloping lot

Winging aloft from either end of this two story home, the balconies become observation towers enhanced by a sharply sloping lot. Skirting the balconies and enjoying the view are the formal dining room, the living room and two of the bedrooms. A family room on the lower level is furnished with its own bath and opens to the covered terrace, where smokeless outdoor cooking is made possible by the vented grill. A carport, large utility room and plentiful storage comprise this level. No. 9806.

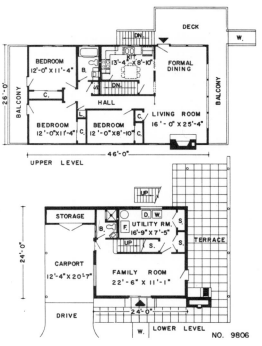

AREA	SQ. FT.
Upper level	—1,196
Lower level	— 576
Carport	— 295

Trailtown

Many building sites are situated so that it is possible to have an excellent view from both front and back of the house. This home has been designed with that thought in mind as you will note from the large window area in the living and dining rooms. A living room such as this one offers numerous possibilities for furniture arrangement and decorating schemes. No. 8110.

AREA	SQ. FT.
First floor	—1,393
Basement	—1,393
Garage	— 300

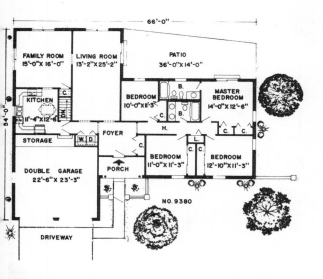

Robinson

Interior Rivals Dramatic Facade

One story traditional displays an eye-catching roof and porch treatment that is rivaled by a luxurious, adaptable interior. With the two end bedrooms, to be added in the future, the design shows a total of four bedrooms and two full baths. An elegant foyer, sweeping living room, eat-in kitchen and family room are additional bonuses. No. 9380.

AREA	SQ. FT.
Living area	—1,512
End bedrooms	— 420

Suburban

Brick chimney asserts individuality

Simple lines are given excitement by the proud brick chimney that slashes the facade of this moderate ranch style. Originality is emphasized on the inside as well, beginning in the living room, where a wood-burning fireplace and sunny picture window radiate atmosphere. A formal dining room skirts the kitchen, which has access to a utility room with half-bath, a choice location for a laundry center. Unique for a home of this size are two full baths, one private to the master bedroom, and adequate closet space. No. 102.

AREA	SQ. FT.
First floor	—1,376

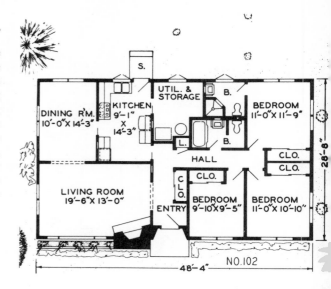

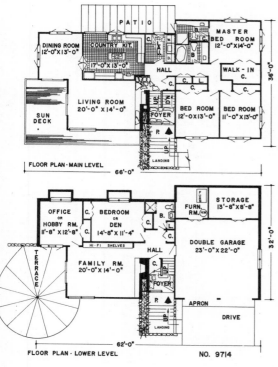

FLOOR PLAN · MAIN LEVEL

DINING ROOM 12'-0" X 13'-0"
PATIO
COUNTRY KIT. 17'-0" X 13'-0"
MASTER BED ROOM 12'-0" X 14'-0"
HALL
WALK-IN C.
SUN DECK
LIVING ROOM 20'-0" X 14'-0"
FOYER
BED ROOM 12'-0" X 13'-0"
BED ROOM 11'-0" X 13'-0"
UP
DN
LANDING
66'-0"
36'-0"

FLOOR PLAN · LOWER LEVEL

OFFICE OR HOBBY RM. 11'-8" X 12'-8"
BEDROOM OR DEN 14'-8" X 11'-4"
HI-FI SHELVES
STORAGE 13'-8" X 8'-8"
FURN. RM.
DOUBLE GARAGE 23'-0" X 22'-0"
HALL
TERRACE
FAMILY RM. 20'-0" X 14'-0"
FOYER
APRON
DRIVE
UP
DN
LANDING
62'-0"
32'-0"

NO. 9714

Oldbury

An impressive split foyer is provided in this attractive hillside home. The lot shown drops eight feet from rear to front but by making minor alterations a more gentle slope can be utilized. Both the living room and dining room have access to the sundeck through sliding glass doors. An excellent floor plan provides many desirable features. The country kitchen has an island type built-in range, built-in desk, freezer and eating space. Two full baths are located in the bedroom area. The master bedroom has an extra large walk-in closet. The lower level provides plenty of space for family activities and entertaining. No. 9714.

AREA	SQ. FT.
Main level	—1,748
Lower level	— 932
Garage	— 768

Oldbury 107

Wentworth

A Stately Home . . .

A charming English Tudor adaptation which retains the appeal of yesteryear, yet features an outstanding contemporary floor plan. There are three large bedrooms, each with a closet over seven feet long. The living room has a wood-burning fireplace, a square bay window and an ornamental iron railing which runs along the stairway and entry. There is eating space in the kitchen for breakfast and snacks. A formal dining room opens onto an elevated wood deck through sliding glass doors. A huge family room, which has a wood-burning fireplace, is located on the lower level as well as a half bath, utility room, shop and double garage. No. 9332.

AREA	SQ. FT.
Upper level	—1,633
Lower level	— 858
Garage and shop	— 718

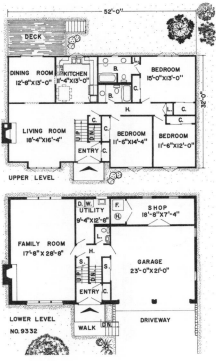

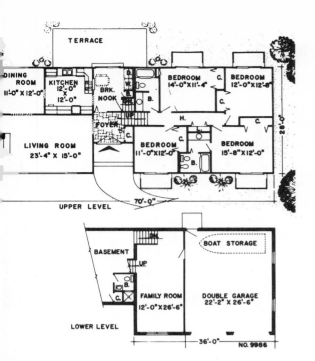

Floor Plan Labels

Upper Level:
- TERRACE
- DINING ROOM 11'-0" X 12'-0"
- KITCHEN 12'-0" X 12'-0"
- BRK. NOOK
- LIVING ROOM 23'-4" X 15'-0"
- FOYER
- BEDROOM 14'-0" X 11'-4"
- BEDROOM 12'-0" X 12'-8"
- BEDROOM 11'-0" X 12'-0"
- BEDROOM 15'-8" X 12'-0"
- 70'-0"
- 28'-0"

UPPER LEVEL

Lower Level:
- BASEMENT
- UP
- BOAT STORAGE
- FAMILY ROOM 12'-0" X 26'-6"
- DOUBLE GARAGE 22'-2" X 26'-6"
- 36'-0"   NO. 9986

LOWER LEVEL

Epernay

Private Balconies Benefit Bedrooms

Four generous bedrooms each open to private balconies via sliding glass doors in this mansard roofed design. Split level zones sleeping rooms for quiet and relaxation, and two full baths serve the area. Overlooking the terrace, a breakfast nook extends the kitchen and combines dining and closed-off laundry areas. Restful log fires brighten the living room, which adjoins a formal dining room. On the lower level, an elongated family room merits a full bath, and double garage assigns boat storage. No. 9986.

AREA	SQ. FT.
Upper levels	—2,080
Family room	— 364
Garage	— 644
Basement	—1,072

Olean

Romantic balcony distinguishes design

Laced with a wrought iron railing, the decorative balcony in this design provides an enchanting contrast to the simple lines of the shutter and brick trimmed exterior. Considerable space is allotted for the foyer, hallway, and curved stairway, achieving a gracious entrance. An unusually large living room is furnished with folding doors that allow it to be closed off for entertaining, and an informal family room adjoins its own full bath. The elongated kitchen provides a breakfast area, and a formal dining room and den are also included. No. 9032.

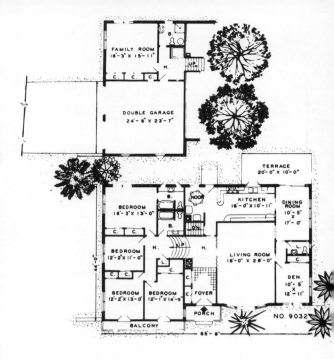

AREA	SQ. FT.
Living areas	—2,704
Garage level	—1,157

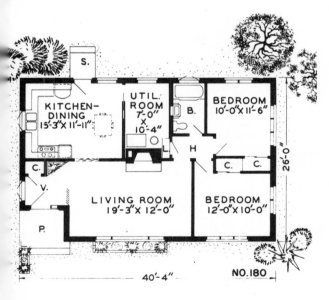

Oliver

Hipped roof, fireplace lend appeal

Exuding comfort and cozy warmth, this small stone design is enhanced by a hipped roof outside and fireplace within. A small family or retired couple will appreciate the interior arrangement. A utility room adjoining the kitchen provides space for laundry facilities close to the area where they are needed. Two bedrooms share the full hall bath, and the substantial kitchen apportions a dining area. The living room, complete with picture windows, affords a cheerful spot for relaxing around the fireplace. No. 180.

AREA	SQ. FT.
First floor	—1,014

Evanston

Angular Beauty Characterizes Design

Bluntly attractive, this contemporary plan combines stark, angular facade with spacious, airy interior. Bedrooms are featured, and a distinctive master bedroom boasts double closets, bath, dressing room, exercise room, and sauna. Upstairs bedrooms merit balconies, and a total of three full baths serve the plan. Sewing room and hobby room on second floor promise extra sleeping space if needed. Set apart for quiet and formality, the living room is noise-buffered by stairs and hallway. No. 10082.

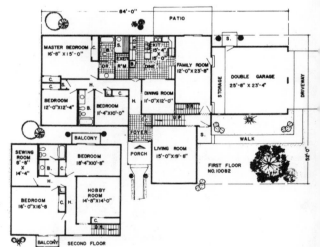

AREA	SQ. FT.
First floor	—2,212
Second floor	—1,206
Garage	— 624
Basement	—1,856

Fenway

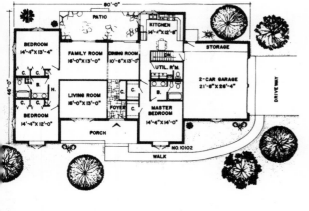

English Tudor Adds Bedrooms, Garage

Either the double garage or two bedrooms and central bath can constitute expansion plans for this brick and stucco Tudor design. In the remaining living space, the emphasis is on luxury, with the tiled foyer allowing access to separate living, dining, and family rooms. The sizable master bedroom is indulged with two walk-in closets and a compartmented bath. No. 10102.

AREA	SQ. FT.
Living area	—1,492
End bedrooms	— 612
Garage	— 616

Dartmouth

Graceful colonial lodges three bedrooms

Colonial detailing, a cupola, and an outstanding garage treatment give this three bedroom home an appealing dignity. Tiny touches of luxury, such as the master bedroom's half bath and the living room's lovely bay window and fireplace typify the interior. A substantial kitchen places its eating area by the window overlooking the porch, and the extended garage borders a sizable storage room. No. 10004.

AREA	SQ. FT.
First floor	—1,008
Basement	—1,008
Garage	— 392

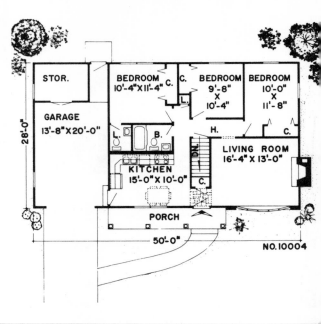

Tahoe

Spanish theme carried throughout

This Spanish ranch design includes such typical details as stucco and brick walls, exposed rough rafter ends, an entrance arch and a sloping fireplace chimney. The Spanish theme is extended inside the house to include a high sloping foyer ceiling with exposed rough beams. There are four bedrooms and two full baths. A combination half-bath/laundry serves the kitchen area and also opens into the hall. A wood-burning fireplace is located in the living room. Sliding glass doors in the family room open onto a large terrace at the rear. A full basement is included. No. 10046.

AREA	SQ. FT.
First floor	—1,885
Basement	—1,885
Garage	— 456

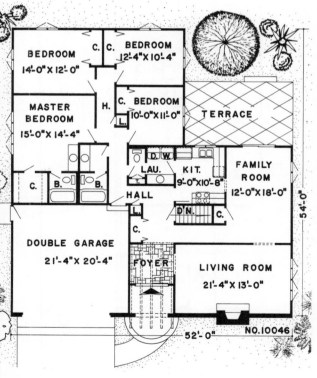

BEDROOM
14'-0" X 12'-0"

C. C. BEDROOM
12'-4" X 10'-4"

MASTER BEDROOM
15'-0" X 14'-4"

H. C. BEDROOM
10'-0" X 11'-0"

TERRACE

C. B. B.

D.W.

LAU. KIT.
9'-0" X 10'-8"

FAMILY ROOM
12'-0" X 18'-0"

HALL

DN. C.

DOUBLE GARAGE
21'-4" X 20'-4"

FOYER

LIVING ROOM
21'-4" X 13'-0"

54'-0"

52'-0" NO. 10046

Sena

Practical baths open to hall, bedrooms

Two functional baths that conveniently open to hall and bedroom reveal the emphasis on livability in this split foyer design. The opulent master bedroom is arranged so that it can be transformed into two bedrooms or divided with a folding door if desired. Walk-in closets offer superior closet space, and a useful breakfast bar swings into the kitchen. Living and dining area is extended by the elevated wooden deck, accessible to the kitchen. A closeted family room and den and a full bath benefit the lower level. No. 9836.

AREA	SQ. FT.
Upper level	—1,586
Lower level	—1,500

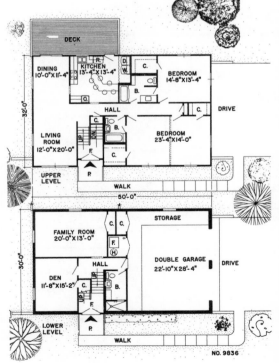

Southwood

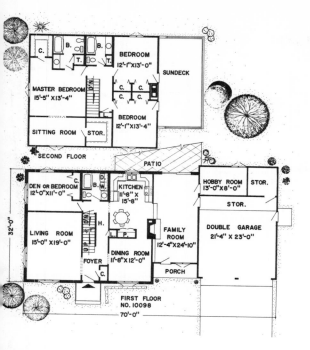

Family room given outside entrance

Sunken family room, spanning the width of this luxurious design to open to patio, enjoys wood-burning fireplace and private outside entrance for convenience and practicality. Above the family room, an extensive sun deck is shared by two bedrooms, while the opulent master bedroom contains sitting room, full bath and huge walk-in closet. Gracious foyer channels traffic to formal living or dining room, and extensive kitchen also adds a dining nook. Hobby room and storage are provided behind the double garage, and extra bedroom and bath are provided on the first floor. No. 10098.

AREA	SQ. FT.
First floor	—1,464
Second floor	—1,152
Basement	—1,152
Garage, hobby and storage	— 704

Drayton

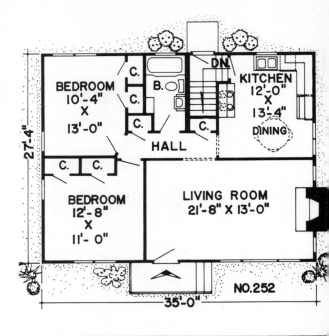

Stone chimney adorns miniature bungalow

Proudly sporting its stone chimney, this tiny home with less than 1000 feet of living area, provides true comfort for a small family. The two bedrooms boast two closets each and share a large bath. The living area, over 21 feet wide and completely separate from the dining area, enjoys a wood-burning fireplace. No. 252.

AREA	SQ. FT.
First floor	— 959
Basement	— 959

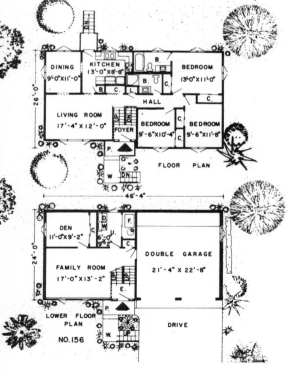

Carnaby

Folding doors valuable addition

Allowing the kitchen and coat closet to be closed off from the living room, the folding doors are one of the thoughtful additions that make this split foyer plan desirable. Besides the formal living room and dining room, a spacious family room is planned for family activities, and the well-closeted den might serve as a study, television room, or extra bedroom. Additional assets are the master bedroom with private bath, the extra large double garage, and the efficient kitchen with built-in broom closet. No. 156.

AREA	SQ. FT.
Upper level	—1,156
Lower level	— 583
Garage	— 528

Stinson

Two decks embrace nature

Built around and into its surroundings, this three bedroom design features an exterior that blends with nature and double decks to embrace it. Living and dining rooms encircle one deck, opening through three sets of sliding glass doors, while another deck opens exclusively to the master bedroom. Favored with walk-in closet and full bath, the master bedroom is set apart for privacy. Two other bedrooms, a hall bath and laundry room complete the plan, and a large detached double garage is provided. No. 10284.

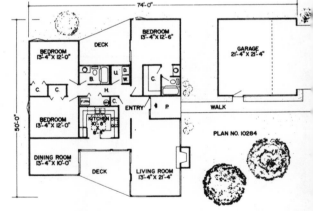

AREA	SQ. FT.
First floor	—1,568
Garage	— 484

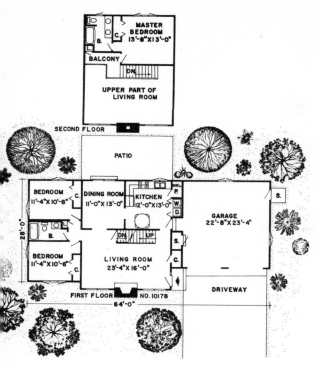

Neptune

Living room lifts, expands design

Airy expansiveness is achieved in this striking design through its generously glassed two story living room, complete with wood-burning fireplace. For effect, the luxurious master bedroom opens to a balcony overlooking the living room. Two bedrooms on the first floor share a full bath. Bordering the opulent living room are the dining room with sliding glass doors to the patio and a kitchen with pantry, laundry niche, and dining area. The attached garage opens to the kitchen. No. 10178.

AREA	SQ. FT.
First floor	1,172
Second floor	— 336
Basement	— 720
Garage	— 576

Watson

Angled design yields interesting shapes

Fresh, innovative planning gives birth to a fascinating and unconventionally shaped kitchen, family room, and dining room in this contemporary design. This unique room arrangement also enjoys sliding glass doors to the partially roofed terrace, where a built-in barbecue grill invites outdoor cooking. The formal, fireplace-brightened living room is free of cross traffic. Three bedrooms comprise the sleeping wing, including a sizable master bedroom with private bath and double closets. No. 140.

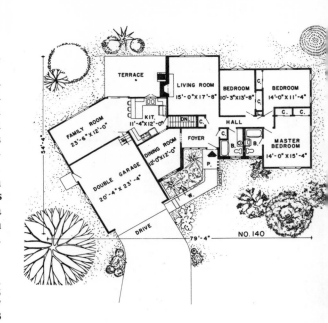

AREA	SQ. FT.
First floor	—1,735
Basement	—1,187
Garage	— 498

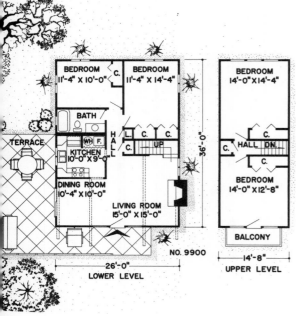

BEDROOM
11'-4" X 10'-0"

BEDROOM
11'-4" X 14'-4"

BATH

TERRACE

KITCHEN
10'-0" X 9'-0"

DINING ROOM
10'-4" X 10'-0"

LIVING ROOM
15'-0" X 15'-0"

HALL

UP

36'-0"

26'-0"
LOWER LEVEL

NO. 9900

BEDROOM
14'-0" X 14'-4"

HALL   DN.

BEDROOM
14'-0" X 12'-8"

BALCONY

14'-8"
UPPER LEVEL

Heiden

Chalet creation sports four bedrooms

Besides the enticing exterior, the main concentration of this chalet design is on sleeping comfort. Four ample bedrooms, one of which opens to a balcony, endow the home with room for a number of guests. Bedrooms and hallways abound with closet space, another valuable contribution to livability. The first floor living room, dining room and kitchen are skirted by the terrace which offers outdoor dining space and is accessible from the dining room through sliding glass doors. No. 9900.

AREA	SQ. FT.
First floor	—936
Second floor	—529

Rock Harbor

Cape Cod design adapts to today

Fully up-to-date, with its luxurious master bedroom and sizable family room, this Cape Cod-inspired home blends warm tradition with a contemporary floor plan. Formal living and dining rooms flank the foyer, and the U-shaped kitchen is handy to dining room and two story family room. For convenience, a large laundry room and half bath are included on this level. Upstairs, the master bedroom enjoys a private bath, dressing area with vanity, and walk-in closet. No. 10280.

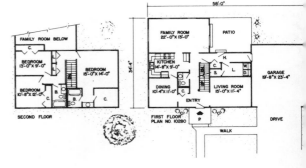

AREA	SQ. FT.
First floor	—1,100
Second floor	— 861
Basement	— 798
Garage	— 481

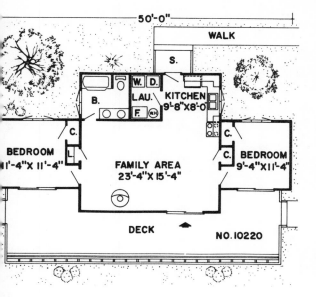

Telluride

Bedrooms merit access to wooden deck

To encourage a relaxed lifestyle and enjoyment of the outdoors, a 50-ft. wooden deck fronts this vacation retreat and opens to two bedrooms as well as the living area. Complete but simple, the plan offers a living area with two closets and a prefab fireplace, open to a compact kitchen with rear entrance. The separate laundry room also houses furnace and water heater, and the large bath features double sinks. The plan can be built without one or both bedrooms if desired. No. 10220.

AREA	SQ. FT.
Family area	—576
Bedroom #1	—168
Bedroom #2	—144
Total	—888

Whitmark

Colonial dignity heightens modern plan

Expressing a traditional warmth through its columned porches and shuttered windows, this three bedroom Colonial arranges a maximum of living space in its one-story plan. Closet space is abundant, both in bedrooms and hallways, and the kitchen allots laundry space and a pantry. Another convenience is the breakfast bar which separates kitchen and family room and is highly useful for snacks and entertaining. Sliding glass doors in the family room open to the large terrace. Two full baths serve the bedroom wing. No. 9280.

AREA	SQ. FT.
First floor	—1,483
Basement	—1,483
Garage	— 422

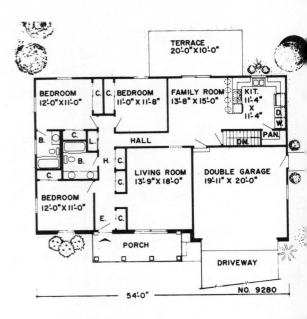

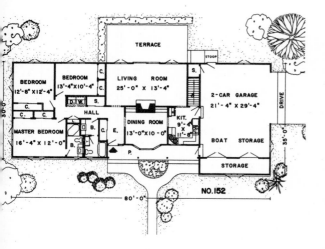

Brighton

Additions transform traditional plan

Intriguing diamond light windows, contrasting siding, and a cupola trim convert this simple ranch style into an appealing design. Its expansive living room enjoys both a fireplace and a terrace, via sliding glass doors. The kitchen is compact and handy to the formal dining room and garage. Three bedrooms comprise the sleeping wing, including a master bedroom with private bath, and a niche is provided for the washer and dryer. Boat storage is included in the extra large garage. No. 152.

AREA	SQ. FT.
First floor	—1,643
Basement	—1,643
Garage	— 763

Eaglescroft

Four bedrooms, library favor tudor plan

Beginning with an elegant foyer and living areas to fill every need, and topped with four large bedrooms, this Tudor-styled design adapts well to a growing family. An appealing combination of stucco, stone, exposed timbers, and multi-lite windows layers the exterior and recalls the past in a charming way. Inside, the traffic pattern creates access to formal living and dining rooms directly off the foyer and informal kitchen, family room, and covered patio beyond. A library is tucked away off the living room. No. 10204.

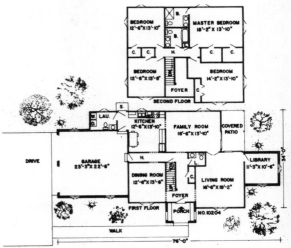

AREA	SQ. FT.
First floor	1,430
Second floor	—1,314
Basement	—1,202
Garage	— 556

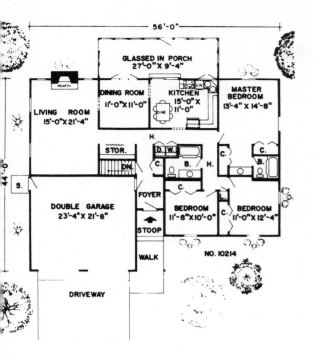

Moorhead

Design focuses on formality

Situated to overlook an impressive 27-ft. glassed-in porch, the dining room joins the formal living room of this ranch plan to create a workable unit for formal entertaining. A cozy fireplace furnishes the living room, and the large kitchen reserves space for family dining. Sizable and well-windowed, the master bedroom offers double closets, dressing area and full bath, and another full bath serves two more bedrooms. For convenience, the double garage opens directly into the foyer. No. 10214.

AREA	SQ. FT.
First floor	—1,651
Basement	—1,651
Garage	— 521

Youngstown

Split level zones living areas

Efficiently zoned space is a main objective of this attractive balconied-split level. Traffic is channeled through the foyer to any of three living areas. To the right, a generous living room shares its wood-burning fireplace with the family room, which overlooks the patio and annexes a powder room. The bedroom wing displays an appealing master bedroom with private bath and balcony. Beneath the bedroom level is a garage large enough for boat storage, a utility room, and a den with adequate closet space. No. 9852.

AREA	SQ. FT.
Living areas	—2,057
Garage-den	— 947
Basement	—1,152

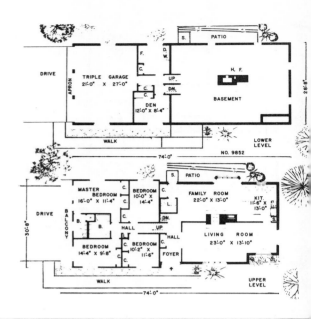

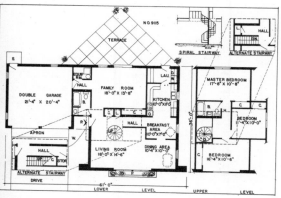

Alyesbury

Move in today—finish it later

This unusual but quite attractive story and
one-half home features a spiral stairway to
the second floor. An alternate is shown for
those that prefer a more conventional stairway. The three bedrooms on the upper level
could be left unfinished by the contractor
and then finished by the man of the house
during his leisure hours. No. 9115.

AREA	SQ. FT.
First floor	—1,185
Second floor	— 549
Garage	— 484

Ashland

Porch, fireplace offer cozy combination

Innovative in approach, this four bedroom contemporary melds a wood-burning fireplace and a screened porch to supply a cozy spot for indoor/outdoor living. Another fireplace brightens the angular living room, open to the porch and to the garden terrace via sliding glass doors and steps from the formal dining room. Carving out a breakfast nook, the corridor kitchen borders a handy laundry room and full bath with shower. Four large bedrooms and two full baths fill the upper level. No. 10216.

AREA	SQ. FT.
First floor	—1,107
Second floor	—1,296
Basement	— 514
Garage	— 530

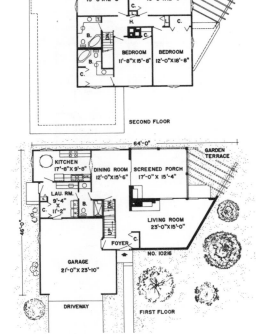

Bellecoeur

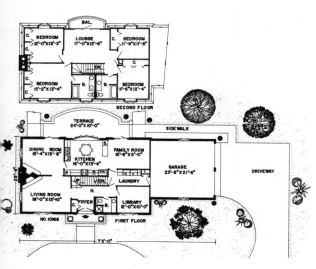

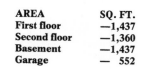

Luxury plan details balconied lounge

Elegantly blending an exterior of brick, shake shingles, and small-paned casement windows, this French country home offers a lavish interior crowned by its 17-foot balconied lounge. Four bedrooms, all with generous closet space, and two large baths also share the second level. Below, the floor plan details an expansive eat-kitchen, family room, laundry center and full bath. Wood-burning fireplaces grace both living and dining room, grouped at left of foyer to insure formality. No. 10166.

AREA	SQ. FT.
First floor	—1,437
Second floor	—1,360
Basement	—1,437
Garage	— 552

Sierra

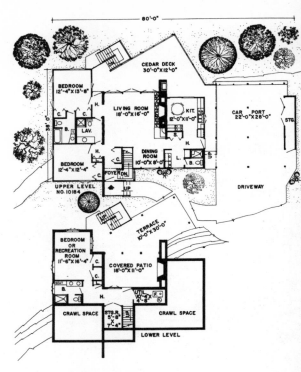

Natural elements mingle in modern plan

Rustic beams, exposed stone, and a cedar deck combine to allow the mingling of indoors and outdoors in this unusual design. Wood-burning fireplaces grace the living room and covered patio, and clerestory windows over the living room promise abundant light and atmosphere. Separated from living areas by an exposed stone wall, the sleeping wing houses two bedrooms and two baths, with another bedroom a possibility on the lower level. The eat-in kitchen opens to the cedar deck via sliding glass doors. No. 10184.

AREA	SQ. FT.
Upper level	—1,500
Lower level	—619

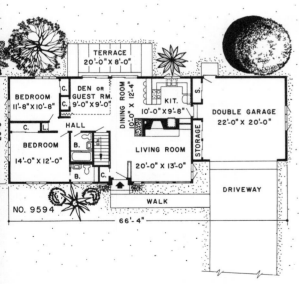

Ranchero

Glass brings the outdoors in . . .

Adaptability is the outstanding characteristic of this modern two bedroom home, and the main evidence is a folding partition wall that can enclose part of the expansive dining room to form a guest room or den. When the partitions are not in use, the living room and dining room, separated from the terrace only by sliding glass doors, offer an immense area for entertaining or relaxing. The kitchen is distinguished by an exposed brick wall which encloses the built-in oven and by the breakfast bar facing the dining area. No. 9594.

AREA	SQ. FT.
First floor	—1,140
Basement	—1,140
Garage	— 462

Keyport

Family, game rooms primed for fun

Sharing an adjacent utility room with sink, freezer and cooktop, the lower level family room and game room occupy a site perfect for entertaining and family recreation. Both rooms are sizable: the game room is large enough to house a pool table, and the family room relaxes with a wood-burning fireplace. This well-balanced split foyer also creates a built-in kitchen with planning desk, formal dining room, and firelit living room. A master bedroom with triple closets and full bath is featured. No. 202.

AREA	SQ. FT.
Upper level	—1,631
Lower level	—1,602
Garage	— 594

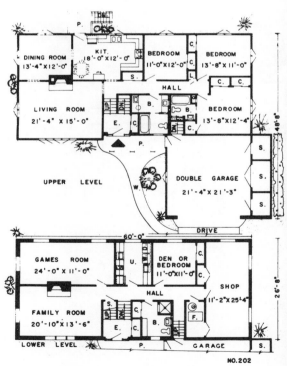

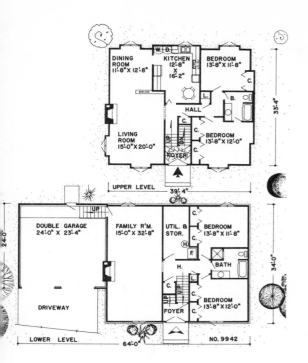

Upper level floor plan:
- DINING ROOM 11'-8" X 12'-8"
- KITCHEN 12'-8" X 16'-2"
- W. D.
- BEDROOM 13'-8" X 11'-8"
- SHELVES
- HALL
- B.
- C.
- L.
- LIVING ROOM 15'-0" X 20'-0"
- BEDROOM 13'-8" X 12'-0"
- FOYER
- C.

UPPER LEVEL
33'-4"
39'-4"

Lower level floor plan:
- DOUBLE GARAGE 24'-0" X 23'-4"
- FAMILY R'M. 15'-0" X 32'-8"
- UTIL. & STOR.
- BEDROOM 13'-8" X 11'-8"
- H.
- E
- H.
- BATH
- DRIVEWAY
- BEDROOM 13'-8" X 12'-0"
- FOYER
- C.

LOWER LEVEL
24'-0"
34'-0"
64'-0"
NO. 9942

Rowley

This unique split foyer design contains a lot of living space. All of the rooms are extra large. Four bedrooms and two full baths are included. The kitchen has plenty of cabinets, washer and dryer space and a breakfast nook. Wood burning fireplaces are found in both the living room and the huge family room. The roof and exterior walls are covered with Red Cedar shake shingles, providing a rustic low maintenance exterior. No. 9942.

AREA	SQ. FT.
Upper level	—1,373
Lower level	—1,309
Garage	— 576

Worchester

This beautiful symmetrical Colonial style home will be an asset to any community. The lavish front entrance, stately columns, prominent bay windows and Old English brick will bring an exclamation of praise from all observers. The floor plan is well arranged and a minimum amount of waste space is present. The garage entrance can be installed at the rear if practical. No. 9221.

AREA	SQ. FT.
First floor	—1,812
Basement	—1,812
Garage	— 630

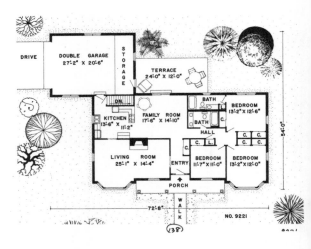

Gironde

Sunlit deck extends living room

Sliding glass doors separate the living room and the expansive sun deck, with privacy assured by four foot high sidewalls. A clever use of space above the garage, the sun deck more than doubles the living room's area for entertaining and relaxing. Wood-burning fireplaces benefit both the living room and immense family room, which opens to a terrace. Three full baths and four bedrooms are included in the plan, as well as a sizable den and storage closet on the lower level. No. 9936.

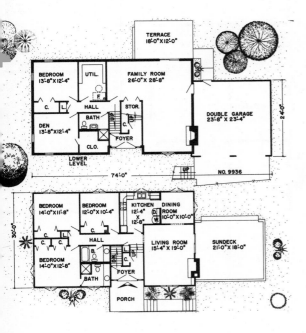

AREA	SQ. FT.
Upper level	—1,480
Lower level	—1,480
Garage	— 576

New Orleans

Two story classic suits large family

A traditional mixture of stately columns and shutters crafts a classic home in this plan, a two story plan for the large family. Four bedrooms and two full baths are provided, and storage closets are generously sprinkled throughout the home. Kitchen and dining are cleaved by a handy snack bar, a closeted entry directs traffic, and the large living room promises a wood-burning fire-place. No. 24052.

AREA	SQ. FT.
First floor	**—768**
Second floor	**—768**
Basement	**—768**
Garage	**—384**

Second Floor

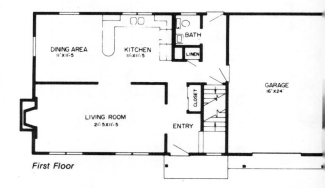

First Floor

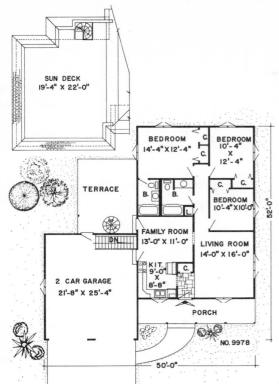

Quillan

Sun deck crowns rustic exterior

Rough cedar plywood battened siding joined with a shake shingle mansard roof radiate a rusticity that is appropriately topped with a large sun deck over the garage. Befitting either a lakeshore, mountain or urban lot, this three bedroom home also details a ground level terrace with staircase spiraling upward to the sun deck. The family room opens to both garage and terrace, and the formal living room looks out on the shaded front porch. No. 9978.

AREA	SQ. FT.
First floor	—1,176
Basement	—1,176
Garage	— 572

Rustic

Building A-frame can be weekend project

Easy to apply red cedar shake shingles are specified roof of this A-frame cabin and help make building it yourself a feasible and rewarding weekend project. Constructed on a concrete slab, the cabin exudes relaxed informality through the warm natural tones of exposed beams and unfinished wood interior. No. 7664.

AREA	SQ. FT.
Main floor	—560
Upper level	—240

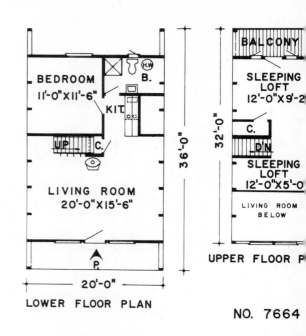

LOWER FLOOR PLAN

BEDROOM 11'-0"X11'-6"

KIT.

UP

C.

LIVING ROOM 20'-0"X15'-6"

36'-0"

20'-0"

P.

BALCONY

SLEEPING LOFT 12'-0"X9'-2

C.

DN

SLEEPING LOFT 12'-0"X5'-0

LIVING ROOM BELOW

32'-0"

UPPER FLOOR P

NO. 7664

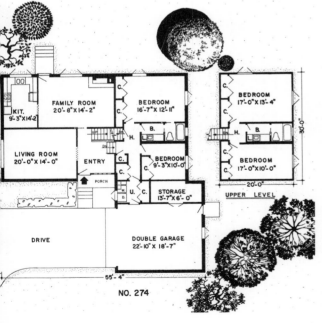

Smithston

Large entrance to living area

Cathedral ceilings and expanses of sidelights create a sensational effect in the entrance foyer of this handsome contemporary split level. To the left, an untrafficked living room is dealt sizable dimensions and supplemented by an even larger family room with fireplace. Rectangular kitchen allows for the installation of snack bar or planning desk. Four bedrooms, two on each level, are completed by two compartmented baths and bountiful closet space. Utility room and storage border the double garage. No. 274.

AREA	SQ. FT.
Living area	—1,573
Upper area	— 600
Basement	— 910
Garage and	
storage	— 560

Morningside

Fireplace breathes life into room

Laced with intriguing diamond light windows, the living room of this well-proportioned plan catches light and life from the wood-burning fireplace. The informal family room merits sliding glass doors which open to the terrace and borders the kitchen with breakfast bar, laundry area, and pantry. Closet space is generously sprinkled throughout the house, especially in the master bedroom. Double sinks benefit the half bath which serves two more bedrooms. No. 9296.

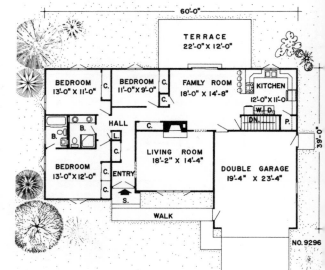

AREA	SQ. FT.
First floor	—1,522
Basement	—1,522
Garage	— 470

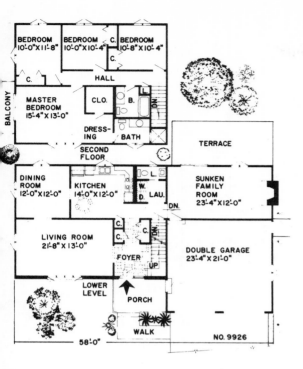

BEDROOM 10'-0"X11'-8" BEDROOM 10'-0"X10'-4" C. BEDROOM 10'-8"X10'-4"

C.

BALCONY

HALL

C.

MASTER BEDROOM 15'-4"X13'-0"

CLO. B. DN.

DRESS-ING BATH

SECOND FLOOR

TERRACE

DINING ROOM 12'-0"X12'-0" KITCHEN 14'-0"X12'-0"

W. D. LAU.

SUNKEN FAMILY ROOM 23'-4"X12'-0"

DN.

LIVING ROOM 21'-8"X13'-0"

C. C. C. C.

FOYER UP

DOUBLE GARAGE 23'-4"X21'-0"

LOWER LEVEL

PORCH

WALK

58'-0"

NO. 9926

Maisland

Floor plan rivals unique exterior

Intriguing stone trim and an ornamental balcony create an exceptional exterior for this two-story traditional with an equally appealing floor plan. A luxurious master bedroom suite incorporates a dressing area, full bath and walk-in closet, and opens to a private balcony via sliding glass doors. No. 9926.

AREA	SQ. FT.
First floor	—1,203
Second floor	— 960
Basement	— 906
Garage	— 505

Quadella

Balconied bedroom dominates design

Layered with shake shingles and brick, this triple-winged design is distinguished by its large and completely private master bedroom suite. Incorporating a compartmented bath and bountiful closet space, the master bedroom opens via sliding glass doors to balconies on either end. On the main level, fireplaces grace the living room and family room, and three bedrooms share two baths, with a powder room conveniently placed near the foyer. A formal dining room augments the eating space provided in the kitchen. No. 9938.

AREA	SQ. FT.
First floor	—2,338
Second floor	— 602
Garage	— 614
Basement	—2,334

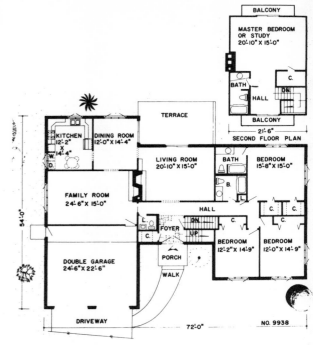

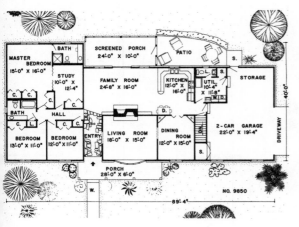

St. Charles

Home recalls southern plantation

Magnificent white columns, shutters, and small paned windows combine to create images of the pre-Civil War South in this generously proportioned design. Inside, the opulent master bedroom suite, with plentiful closet space, a full bath and study, suggests modern luxury. Fireplaces enhance the formal living room and sizable family room, which skirts the lovely screened porch. The formal dining room boasts built-in china closets, and a laundry room and half bath border the kitchen. Liberal storage space is provided in the double garage. No. 9850.

AREA	SQ. FT.
First floor	—2,466
Basement	—1,337
Garage	— 644

Villa Bella

Sumptuous plan begins with courtyard

Arched entrances, courtyard, and garden spark an immediate welcome in this lavish Spanish-styled design. Replete with extras like the first floor study, breakfast room and utility/half bath, the plan combines luxury and livability. The family room stretches nearly 29 feet and offers fireplace and sliding glass doors to the patio, while a double-closeted master bedroom merits a private deck. Formal living and dining rooms flank the foyer. No. 10174.

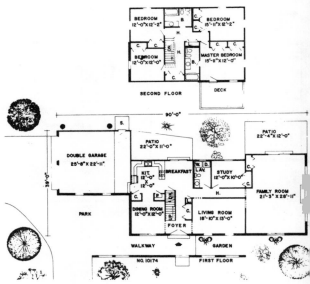

AREA	SQ. FT.
First floor	—1,830
Second floor	—1,171
Basement	—1,176
Garage	— 634

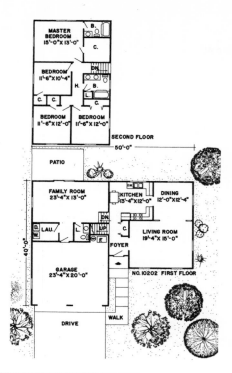

MASTER
BEDROOM
15'-0" X 13'-0"

BEDROOM
11'-6" X 10'-4"

BEDROOM
11'-6" X 12'-0"

BEDROOM
11'-6" X 12'-0"

SECOND FLOOR

50'-0"

PATIO

FAMILY ROOM
23'-4" X 13'-0"

KITCHEN
13'-4" X 12'-0"

DINING
12'-0" X 12'-4"

LAU.

LIVING ROOM
19'-4" X 15'-0"

FOYER

GARAGE
23'-4" X 20'-0"

NO. 10202 FIRST FLOOR

DRIVE

WALK

Walden

Trim split level sports practical plan

Sheathed in a shake shingled mansard roof
and battened plywood siding, this neat split
level features a floor plan based on practicality. Formal areas are clustered on the entry
level, where a closeted foyer greets guests
and channels traffic to living room or dining
room. At the end of the hallway, the eat-in
kitchen stands ready to serve the formal
dining room or the family room, set apart on
a lower level. A sleeping wing occupies the
level above and includes four sizable bedrooms and two full baths. No. 10202.

AREA	SQ. FT.
First floor	—1,172
Second floor	— 960
Garage	— 408

San Souci

Patio contains built-in barbecue

Shake shingles, battened siding and natural stone are skillfully blended together to produce a beautiful facade for this home. The traffic pattern permits access to all rooms from the foyer without crossing another room. Sliding glass doors in the family room, dinette and master bedroom open onto the large patio-pool area. The built-in barbecue on the patio is roofed to provide a shaded area near the pool. No. 10064.

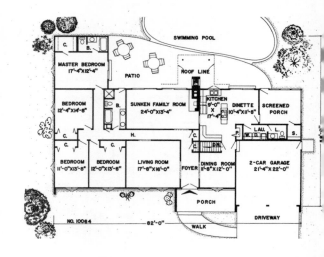

AREA	SQ. FT.
First floor	—2,585
Basement	—2,585
Garage	— 493

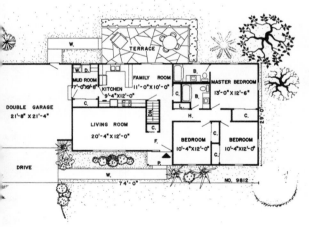

Foxridge

Mud room separates garage, kitchen

Gardening and woodworking tools will find a home in the storage closet of the useful mud room in this rustic detailed ranch. Besides incorporating a laundry area, the mud room will prove invaluable as a place for removing snowy boots and draining wet umbrellas. The family room appendages the open kitchen and flows outward to the stone terrace. The master bedroom is furnished with private bath and protruding closet space, and the living room retains a formality by being situated by itself to the left of the entryway. No. 9812.

AREA	SQ. FT.
First floor	—1,396
Basement	—1,396
Garage	— 484

Faemouth

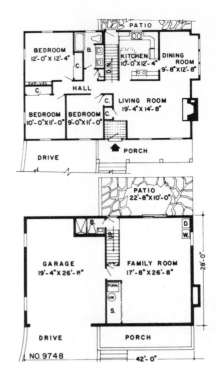

Pillars express charm, welcome

Stately white pillars add a Colonial charm and suggest welcome in this comfortable three bedroom design. Besides the attractive front porch, the plan boasts a sizable living room with fireplace and a separate dining room, one side of which is lined with windows. The bedroom wing includes three bedrooms, one with built-in shelves, and an elongated bath furnished with a linen closet and double sinks. Downstairs, the extensive family room enjoys a full bath with shower and access to the patio. No. 9748.

AREA	SQ. FT.
First floor	—1,200
Basement	—1,176

Graycliff

Lavish plan exercise in luxury . . .

From its impressive facade to its smallest details, this cut stone two story home expresses luxury. Four bedrooms include a first floor master bedroom suite indulged with two private baths, two walk-in closets, and adjoining 27-foot library. Firelit living room rises two stories for a dramatic effect and, with the cozy den with built-in bar, opens to the long balcony. Patio, deck, and pool are outlined for the rear yard, and useful half bath, dressing rooms and sauna complete the basement level. The breakfast room opens to a screened porch, and utility room and triple garage are featured. No. 20006.

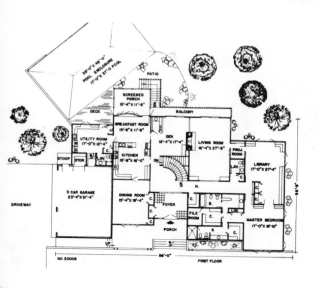

AREA	SQ. FT.
First floor	—3,975
Second floor	—2,205
Basement	—3,975
Garage	— 753

Four Winds

Double decks benefit two story

Serving first floor kitchen and dining room and two second floor bedrooms, the double decks become practical and appealing elements in this angular contemporary. Living areas zone themselves by extending in three directions on the first level, and bedrooms maintain privacy in the same way on the level above. Besides the half bath bordering the utility room, the design shows two full baths, one with a dressing area off the master bedroom. A snack bar is featured in the kitchen. No. 10278.

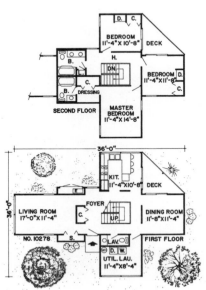

AREA	SQ. FT.
First floor	— 904
Second floor	— 768

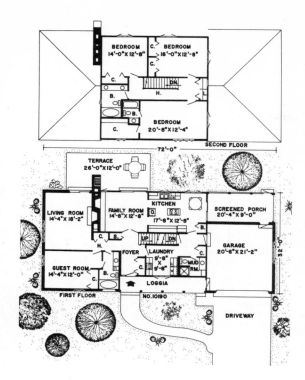

Carlenton

Guest room, four baths equip home

Generous amounts of living space characterize this expansive plan, which enjoys such bonuses as a guest room, screened porch, mud room, and four full baths. Beginning with the generous foyer, the living level houses rooms to accommodate the various activities of a large family. Laundry and mud room are convenient to the 17-ft. kitchen, which opens to the screened porch, while living and family rooms merit fireplaces and sliding glass doors to the terrace. The upstairs bedroom unit is highlighted by the huge master bedroom with walk-in closet and private bath. No. 10190.

AREA	SQ. FT.
First floor	—1,493
Second floor	—1,111
Basement	— 944
Garage	— 481

Yellowstone

Fireplaces illuminate three rooms

Glowing embers set the mood in three rooms of this distinctive split foyer design. Besides the wood burning fireplace in the family room, a two-way fireplace is shared by the living room and formal dining room on the upper level. This level also houses a sizable kitchen with dining space and broom closet, and two bedrooms, one with private balcony, as well as an extended compartmented bath. The lower level incorporates two more bedrooms, a bath, den and family room. No. 9268.

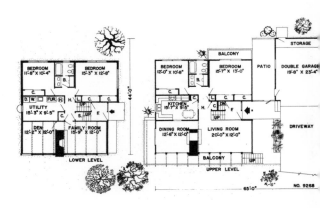

AREA	SQ. FT.
Upper level	—1,268
Lower level	—1,216
Garage	— 487

Roxanne

Balconied suite awesome climax

Eight foot wide glass doors open onto the balcony framing the front of this impressive second floor suite. Perfect for an artist's studio, the suite would also yield a luxurious master bedroom complex, since it houses a bountiful walk-in closet and compartmented bath. Below, the sunken living room boasts a wood-burning fireplace that can be savored from the dining room, and a wooden deck underlies the California room at front, with shrubbery providing privacy. This level quarters four bedrooms and two and one half baths, including the family room's private baths. No. 9958.

AREA	SQ. FT.
First floor	—2,426
Second floor	— 520
Basement	—2,426
Garage	— 572

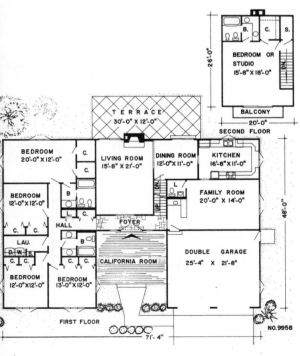

SECOND FLOOR

BEDROOM OR STUDIO 15'-8" X 18'-0"

BALCONY

26'-0"

20'-0"

FIRST FLOOR

NO. 9958

TERRACE 30'-0" X 12'-0"

BEDROOM 20'-0" X 12'-0"

LIVING ROOM 15'-8" X 21'-0"

DINING ROOM 12'-0" X 11'-0"

KITCHEN 16'-8" X 11'-0"

BEDROOM 12'-0" X 12'-0"

FAMILY ROOM 20'-0" X 14'-0"

HALL

FOYER

LAU.

CALIFORNIA ROOM

DOUBLE GARAGE 25'-4" X 21'-8"

BEDROOM 12'-0" X 12'-0"

BEDROOM 13'-0" X 12'-0"

48'-0"

71'-4"

Dartwood

Balcony, lounge grace two story plan

Furnished with a cozy wood-burning fireplace, the 16-ft. lounge on the upper level of this Early American design also enjoys access to the functional balcony. Three large bedrooms are included on this level, which overlooks the impressive two story foyer. Below, the plan etches rooms for all purposes. Formal living and dining rooms augment the casual family room which opens to the patio. Another patio joins the heavily-glassed breezeway, and breakfast nook, half bath, and laundry are bonuses. No. 10186.

AREA	SQ. FT.
First floor	—1,392
Second floor	—1,392
Basement	—1,392
Garage	— 617

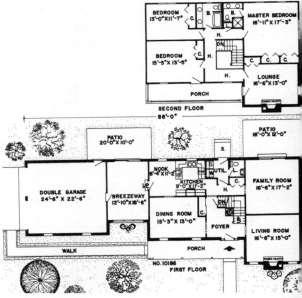

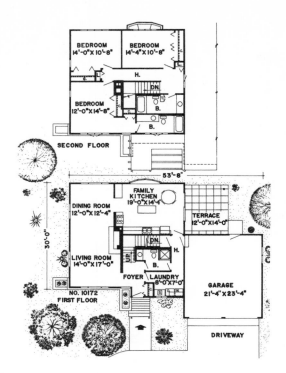

BEDROOM
14'-0" X 10'-8"

BEDROOM
14'-4" X 10'-8"

H.

DN.

B.

BEDROOM
12'-0" X 14'-8"

B.

SECOND FLOOR

53'-8"

FAMILY KITCHEN
19'-0" X 14'-4"

DINING ROOM
12'-0" X 12'-4"

TERRACE
12'-0" X 14'-0"

30'-0"

LIVING ROOM
14'-0" X 17'-0"

UP

DN.

B.

H.

FOYER

LAUNDRY
8'-0" X 7'-0"

GARAGE
21'-4" X 23'-4"

NO. 10172
FIRST FLOOR

DRIVEWAY

Hershell

Two story home eye-catching, practical

Unique and striking on the exterior, this two story home adds interior design elements that result in a highly livable plan. Bonuses, such as the first floor laundry and full bath, are carefully integrated. For character, the fireplace in the living room extends to form a floor-to-ceiling textured masonry wall, and for practicality, the spacious family-kitchen opens to a terrace. Three sizable bedrooms and two full baths comprise the second level. No. 10172.

AREA	SQ. FT.
First floor	—997
Second floor	—960
Garage	—528

Quitman

Design invites formality, relaxation

Both formal and informal areas are outlined in this adaptation of Georgian style architecture. Across the columned porch and into the gracious entry hall, you find immediate access to the elegant living room and adjacent formal dining room. To the right of the entry, however, the family room with fireplace is open to the kitchen, separated only by a breakfast bar. Unusually large closets are found in the bedrooms, especially the master bedroom, which also incorporates, a well-planned bath and dressing area. No. 9282.

AREA	SQ. FT.
First floor	—1,288
Second floor	—1,288
Basement	—1,288
Garage	— 788

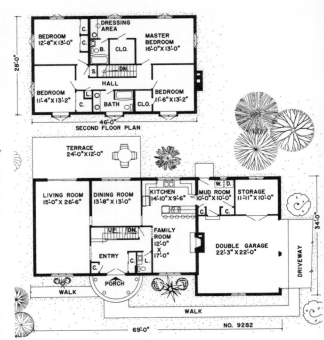

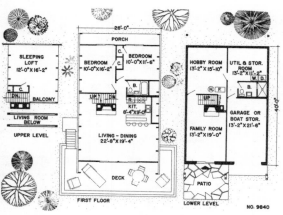

SLEEPING LOFT
12'-0" X 16'-2"

C.

BALCONY

LIVING ROOM BELOW

UPPER LEVEL

PORCH

28'-0"

BEDROOM
10'-0" X 16'-2"

C.
C.

BEDROOM
10'-0" X 11'-6"

B.

UP

R.
KIT.
8'-4" X 9'-0"

LIVING - DINING
22'-8" X 19'-4"

DECK

FIRST FLOOR

40'-0"

HOBBY ROOM
13'-2" X 15'-10"

UTIL & STOR. ROOM
13'-2" X 11'-2"

H F
W. D.

B.

UP

FAMILY ROOM
13'-2" X 19'-0"

GARAGE OR BOAT STOR.
13'-2" X 21'-6"

PATIO

LOWER LEVEL

NO. 9840

Hedmark

Covered patio invites outdoor living

Encircling part of three sides of this home, an expansive sun deck spills off the living and dining room and allows an unparalleled view of lake or mountain surroundings. Beneath the sun deck, a stone patio balances the stone siding of the family room and is reached via sliding glass doors. The first level also includes a large hobby room, utility and storage room and half-bath. Two bedrooms, a full bath, and kitchen with breakfast bar complete the upstairs plan, and a substantial sleeping loft with closet comprise the third level. No. 9840.

AREA	SQ. FT.
First floor	—1,120
Lower level	—1,120
Upper level	— 340

Keltingham

Plan Incorporates English Tudor Appeal

Balancing the traditional English Tudor exterior of this roomy plan is the interior, where the plentiful use of exposed ceiling beams adds interest to the contemporary floor plan. Especially appealing is the first floor master bedroom, indulged with walk-in closet, dressing area, and private bath. Another full bath and laundry room signal convenience on this floor, which also offers a firelit family room, large formal living room, and kitchen with pantry. Upstairs, two more bedrooms are placed to take advantage of the 20-foot deck. No. 10154.

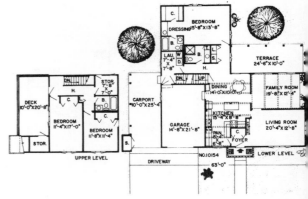

AREA	SQ. FT.
First floor	—1,536
Second floor	— 624
Garage	— 330
Carport	— 253
Basement	— 680

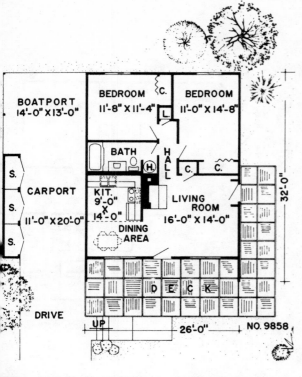

BOATPORT
14'-0" X 13'-0"

BEDROOM
11'-8" X 11'-4"

BEDROOM
11'-0" X 14'-8"

S.

CARPORT

11'-0" X 20'-0"

S.

S.

BATH

HALL

C.

C.

KIT.
9'-0"
X
14'-0"

DINING
AREA

LIVING
ROOM
16'-0" X 14'-0"

32'-0"

DRIVE

UP

26'-0"

NO. 9858

D E C K

Glenview

Cedar shakes both rustic, practical

Red cedar shake shingles that will weather naturally make this design appealing and practical. In the foreground is a large wooden deck which allows entry to the living room. A corner wood-burning fireplace adds a rustic warmth indoors. Two bedrooms, with adequate closet space, a full bath, and kitchen with eating space round out the floor plan. Outside, the attractive shed roof fashions a carport and boatport, with an additional closed storage area along the wall. No. 9858.

AREA	SQ. FT.
First floor	—832
Storage, carport boat port	—448

Westchester

Balcony watchtower to three winds

Encircling the unique living room and family room, the expansive balcony distinguishes this split foyer design and enjoys breezes from three directions. The living room with fireplace melts into the family room and country kitchen. Four bedrooms occupy the sleeping wing and include a master bedroom suite, with dressing room, walk-in closet and compartmented bath. The lower level houses a bedroom and bath and a huge recreation room that spills onto a sunken terrace. No. 9896.

AREA	SQ. FT.
Upper level	—2,269
Lower level	—1,482
Garage	— 806

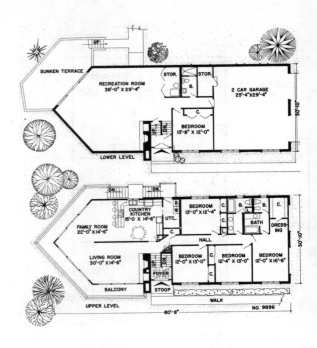

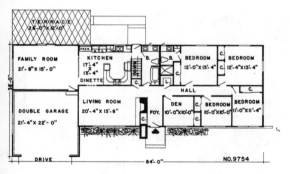

Morna

Active family finds room to live

Open, airy planning and generously proportioned rooms provide a livable setting for an active family in this sprawling ranch plan. Sliding glass doors separate terrace from family room, an expansive area made larger by openness to spacious kitchen, zoned for activity with laundry space and dining area. Completing the area is a living room lighted by wood-burning fireplace. Foyer, stairs and hall buffer noises and separate the sleeping wing, comprising four bedrooms, two baths and a den. No. 9754.

AREA	SQ. FT.
First floor	—2,081
Basement	—1,736
Garage	— 497

Mossridge

Rustic Exterior Layers Expansion Plan

Fieldstone, battened plywood siding, and brick texture this rugged ranch style. As an expansion plan, either the garage or two end bedrooms may be slated for later completion, leaving a roomy two bedroom home featuring covered porch, foyer, and family room with fireplace. Formal living and dining rooms are balanced by informal breakfast room, corridor kitchen, and utility/ half bath. No. 9382.

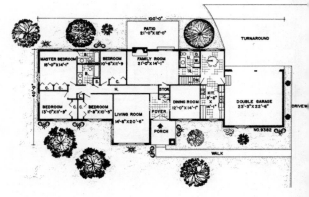

AREA	SQ. FT.
Living area	—1,960

Shelton

Bow Window Whispers Elegance, Style

Trimmed with tradition, this singular split level faces forward its graceful bow window and stately entrance. Inside, the design zones living, sleeping, and recreation areas. Contrasting with the living room's formality, the family room arranges relaxed dining and opens to a spacious terrace. Carefully proportioned bedrooms provide privacy and quiet and share two sizable baths. Another full bath is offered on the lower level as well as a laundry room, recreation room, and hobby room, complete with closet and ready to serve as a bedroom. No. 9255.

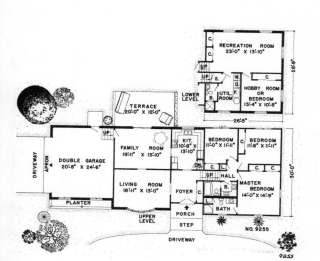

AREA	SQ. FT.
Upper level	—1,624
Lower level	— 758
Garage	— 550

Elkwood

A-Frame garnished with stone chimney

Trimmed with balcony and sun deck and
garnished with a stone chimney, this
A-Frame presents an engaging exterior.
Inside, it is evident that the home is intended
for all season use. A full bath serves each
floor, including the basement which contains
a huge recreation room and boat garage.
No. 9876.

AREA	SQ. FT.
First floor	—1,232
Second floor	— 717
Basement	—1,232

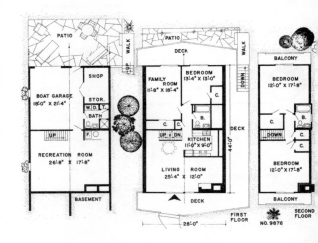

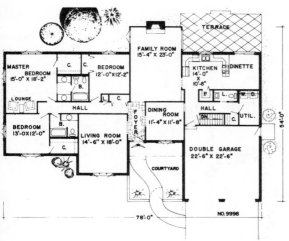

Del Rio

Exterior promise of luxury fulfilled

Graceful Spanish arches and stately brick suggest the rich attention to detail that is found inside this expansive three bedroom home. The plush master bedroom suite, a prime example, luxuriates in a lounge, walk-in closet and private bath. Exposed rustic beams and a cathedral ceiling heighten the formal living room, and an unusually large family room savors a wood-burning fireplace. In addition to the formal dining room, a kitchen with dinette and access to the terrace is planned. No. 9998.

AREA	SQ. FT.
First floor	—2,333
Basement	—1,333
Garage	— 559

Kristian

Dutch Colonial sports space, sun deck

Generously proportioned rooms and an appealing sun deck characterize this sprawling Dutch Colonial design. A perfect structure for the large family, this five bedroom home features, on the entry level, a bedroom, full bath, and laundry, as well as kitchen, dining area and living room. This 27-foot living room enjoys a wood-burning fireplace, and, with the dining area, sliding glass doors to the large roofed terrace. Upstairs, four bedrooms are well supplied with closet space. No. 10160.

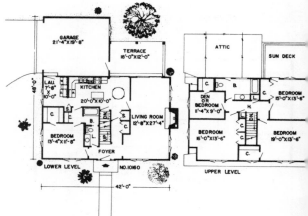

AREA	SQ. FT.
First floor	—1,176
Second floor	—1,176
Basement	—1,176
Garage	— 440

Wyman

Den, breakfast room assets in plan

Combining a cozy traditional facade with plenty of space for family living, this two story design includes a breakfast room on the main floor and den upstairs. From the entry, all areas of the first floor are easily reached, with secluded living room meriting formality and a wood-burning fireplace. The family dining room opens to a semi-private patio, and laundry and half bath are convenient extras. For maximum quiet, three bedrooms are nestled on the second floor, and the master bedroom enjoys a private bath. No. 10276.

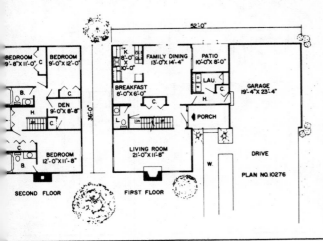

AREA	SQ. FT.
First floor	—877
Second floor	—792
Garage	—480
Basement	—784

Yvette

Semicircular terrace offers access

Spanning four rooms to the rear of the home, the semicircular terrace in this plan is accessible through sliding glass doors from the living room, dining room and family room. The sunken living room with fireplace borders the formal dining room, and a kitchen with laundry space is situated to serve both dining room and family room. Three of the bedrooms, including the master bedroom which merits a bath and large closet, face front and enjoy lovely bay windows. No. 9882.

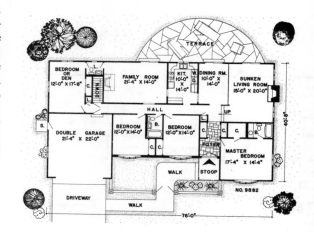

AREA	SQ. FT.
First floor	—2,212
Basement	—2,212
Garage	— 491

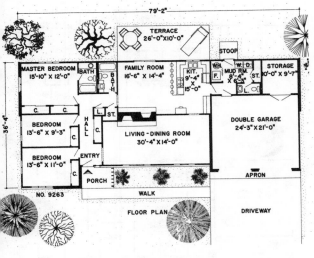

Floor plan labels:

- 79'-2"
- 36'-4"
- TERRACE 26'-0"X10'-0"
- STOOP
- MASTER BEDROOM 15'-10" X 12'-0"
- BATH
- FAMILY ROOM 16'-6" X 14'-4"
- KIT. 9'-4" X 15'-0"
- W.H.
- MUD RM. 8'-4" X 6'-5"
- STORAGE 10'-0" X 9'-7"
- BATH
- F.
- ST.
- C. C.
- BEDROOM 13'-6" X 9'-3"
- L.
- ST.
- C.
- HALL
- LIVING - DINING ROOM 30'-4" X 14'-0"
- DOUBLE GARAGE 24'-3" X 21'-0"
- BEDROOM 13'-6" X 11'-0"
- C.
- ENTRY
- PORCH
- NO. 9263
- WALK
- FLOOR PLAN
- APRON
- DRIVEWAY

Claycourt

This beautiful Ranch design features an extra large living room with plenty of formal dining space at the end. A large wood burning fireplace is found in both the living room and the family room. A long breakfast bar divides the kitchen and family room. The busy housewife will appreciate the mud area. It contains the laundry equipment, a half bath and a large storage closet or pantry. Notice how the bedroom area is zoned away from the rest of the house, thereby providing maximum privacy and quiet. Since the house is basementless, a large storage room behind the garage is provided. No. 9263.

AREA	SQ. FT.
First floor	—1,878
Garage	— 538

Amesbury

Exterior exhibits appealing blend

Rough simplicity expressed by the stone and shutter accents in this Colonial plan vie with graceful bow windows in dominating the handsome exterior. Modern convenience is uppermost in the floor plan, however, which etches four bedrooms and two baths, plus a sizable maid's room and bath. Spanning over 20 feet, the master bedroom is a delightful combination of space, closets, and full bath. Immense and fireplace-brightened, the living room provides a substantial area for formal entertaining and, with the dining room, opens to the terrace. A private garden adjoins the large family room. No. 9913.

AREA	SQ. FT.
First floor	—1,526
Second floor	—1,870
Garage	— 576
Basement	—1,398

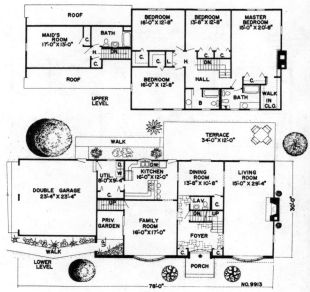

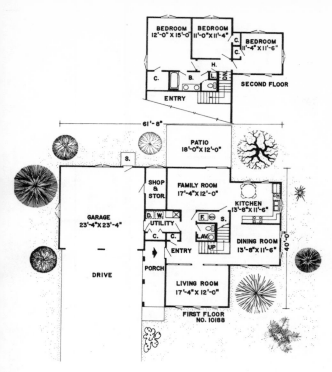

Catskill

Plan offers first floor laundry, shop

Natural wood shapes the exterior of this contemporary design, arranged for living and working. Off the garage, a functional shop provides a haven for the hobbyist, while the utility room houses laundry equipment for step-saving efficiency. Plentiful expanses of glass bathe the home in natural light, and storage space is abundant. Radiating from the well-planned compartmented bath, three bedrooms fill the upper level. Another half bath is featured below, equally convenient to living and family rooms. No. 10188.

AREA	SQ. FT.
First floor	—1,110
Second floor	— 683
Garage and shop—	657

Hancock

Two story colonial emphasizes elegance

Separating formal and informal areas on the main floor, isolating sleeping areas upstairs, this dignified colonial design shows a floor plan adaptable to entertaining and family living. Formal living and dining rooms fill the area to the left of the foyer, while the family room and eat-in kitchen with separate pantry are set at right. A half bath and laundry divide family and dining rooms, each favored with sliding glass doors to the patio. Four bedrooms and two full baths complete the second level. No. 10164.

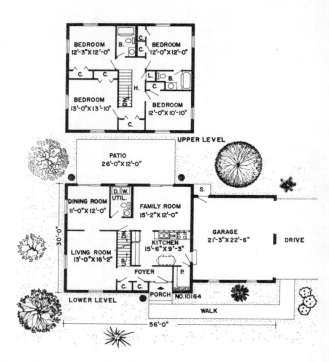

AREA	SQ. FT.
First floor	—1,005
Second floor	—1,020
Basement	—1,005
Garage	— 528

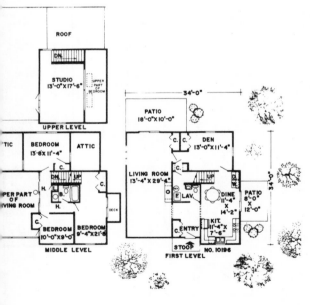

Wheatridge

Vacation retreat captures light, air

Heavily glassed to ensure sunlight and scenery, this three bedroom refuge promises totally comfortable living all year long. The entry level spotlights a 29-ft. living room, open to the patio through sliding glass doors. Another patio annexes the dining area, and a sizable den promises space for reading, watching television, or accommodating extra guests. Nestled in the middle level are three bedrooms, one of which opens to a private deck. The large studio, an undisturbed area for quiet and privacy, tops the design. No. 10196.

AREA	SQ. FT.
Lower level	—1,089
Middle level	— 652
Upper level	— 306

Plumwood

Double-winged plan absorbs scenery

Expanses of glass, especially in living and family rooms, open this two bedroom design to its surroundings. Accessible and attractive, wooden decks encircle the plan, making it an ideal choice for shore or woodland setting. To the right of the closeted entry, the living room stretches over 19 feet to offer space for relaxed conversation and a view. The kitchen is compact and borders a family-dining room, open to the adjoining deck. Two sizable bedrooms are separated by a compartmented full bath. No. 10282.

AREA	SQ. FT.
First floor	—1,136
Basement	
expansion room—	387

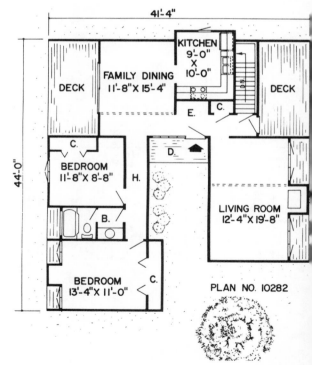

Unberland

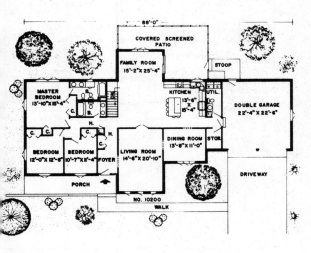

Airy ranch style features screen patio

Open to the family room and steps from the kitchen for cookouts, the covered screened porch provides the perfect accent for this spacious and well-windowed contemporary ranch style. Central foyer and hallway channel traffic to bedrooms, formal living and dining rooms, and the expansive family room-kitchen complex. Serving as a focal point of the plan, the family-kitchen borders a utility room and shows entrances to back yard and garage. Three bedrooms and two full baths make up the sleeping wing. No. 10200.

AREA	SQ. FT.
First floor	—2,254
Basement	—2,134
Garage	—554

Holliver

Porch connects garage, foyer

Accessibility is a prime consideration in this trim three bedroom traditional, where the covered porch connects to the entry to provide shelter, a link to the garage, and a warm welcome. Within steps of the foyer is a formal bow-windowed living room and a well-placed corridor kitchen. Laundry and half bath border the kitchen on one end, while an airy family room at the other end boasts a dining area, storage space, and sliding glass doors to the patio. No. 10212.

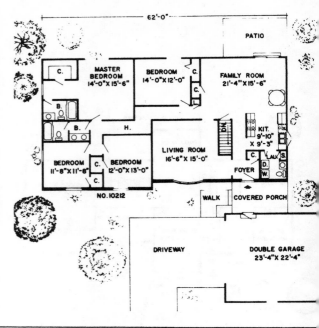

AREA	SQ. FT.
First floor	—2,055
Basement	—2,055
Garage	— 552

Metcalf

Triple-winged Plan Displays Versatility

Three distinct areas in this striking contemporary show its possibilities as an expansion plan. Either the formal living room or the double garage could be completed later without harming the home's livability. Or, two rear bedrooms could be omitted, leaving a bedroom and two baths, a cozy family room, dining room, and kitchen-utility complex. No. 374.

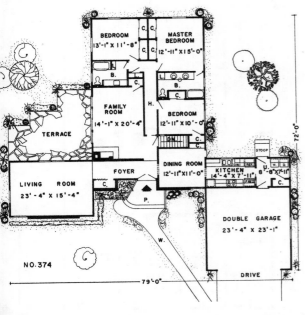

AREA	SQ. FT
Living Area	—1,343
Living Room	— 384
Rear Bedrooms	— 380
Garage	— 552

Allerton

·Bedrooms benefit both levels of plan

Sleek and contemporary, this split foyer plan incorporates two bedrooms and two baths on the upper level and adds another bedroom and den on the lower level. Upstairs, living-dining room stretches over 21 feet and terminates in sliding glass doors to the sunny balcony. Sizable family room provides additional recreation space in an area designed to absorb noise and is bordered by double garage on one side and long utility-storage room on the other. Lower level bath features shower and linen closet. No. 316.

AREA	SQ. FT.
Upper level	—949
Lower level	—949
Garage	—305

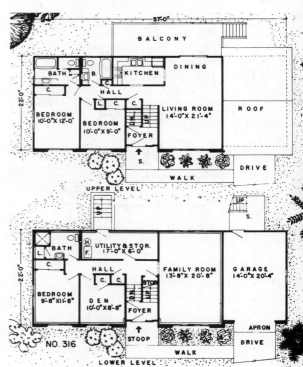

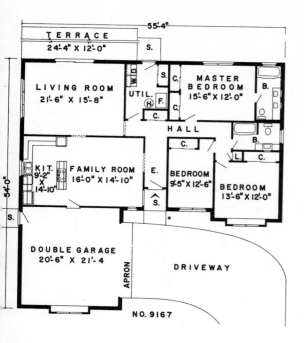

TERRACE 24'-4" X 12'-0"

55'-4"

LIVING ROOM 21'-6" X 15'-8"

UTIL.

MASTER BEDROOM 15'-6" X 12'-0"

HALL

KIT. 9'-2" X 14'-10"

FAMILY ROOM 16'-0" X 14'-10"

BEDROOM 9'-5" X 12'-6"

BEDROOM 13'-6" X 12'-0"

DOUBLE GARAGE 20'-6" X 21'-4

DRIVEWAY

APRON

54'-0"

NO. 9167

Engleside

A great deal of thought and time were spent to produce this beautiful home. Notice how well the exterior colors blend together. This is the result of professional planning. The interior is equally well planned. A perfect traffic pattern permits access to each room without any cross traffic. The living room opens onto the terrace through sliding glass doors. This encourages indoor-outdoor living and will permit the occupants to take advantage of a view or backyard garden. Although no basement is specified, if desired, a stairway can be installed in part of the utility room space. No. 9167.

AREA	SQ. FT.
First floor	—1,808
Garage	— 485

Rociada

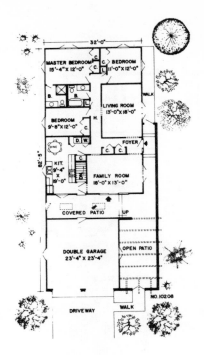

Spanish styling suits narrow lot

Elegant, elongated, and definitely Spanish in origin, this three bedroom home is accented with patios and designed to grace a narrow lot. Front entry garage borders an open patio with arched walkway which preludes entry into the home. Conveniently open to kitchen and family room, a covered patio is sandwiched between garage and living areas for accessible but absolutely private enjoyment of the outdoors. Double closets line the foyer, which is flanked by living and family room. No. 10208.

AREA	SQ. FT.
First floor	—1,600
Basement	—1,600
Garage	— 586

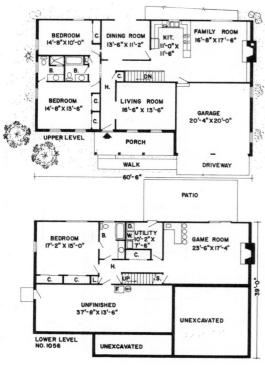

Gentle Oak

Plan custom-designed for sloping lot

Fireplaces and bedrooms on two levels are among the appealing features of this three bedroom traditional, arranged to take advantage of a sloping lot. Built into the hillside, the plan calls for a lower level that is spacious and well-windowed, with large bedroom, utility room, and firelit game room with wet bar. A compartmented full bath opens to bedroom and hallway. On the main living level, formal living and dining rooms balance the airy kitchen/family room combination. No. 1056.

AREA	SQ. FT.
First floor	—1,620
Finished basement	—1,080
Unfinished	— 540
Garage	— 426

Sage

This beautiful two-story home has six bedrooms, three baths with tubs and one bath with a shower. This will comfortably house a large active family. There is an extra large family room which opens onto the terrace through sliding glass doors. A separate dining room is provided for formal occasions. The large double garage opens to the rear but if a corner lot is available, the doors can be installed on the side. A full basement provides space for the utilities, general storage and a recreation room could be finished. No. 9288.

AREA	SQ. FT.
First floor	—1,867
Second floor	—1,152
Basement	—1,872
Garage	— 614

Pipkin

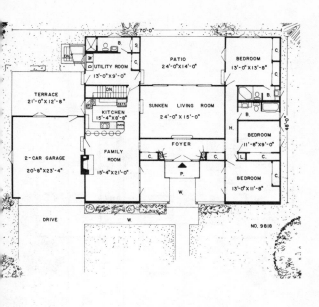

Study this "H" design . . .

The contemporary family looking for a new home that is different from the average, should study this unusual design. The floor plan is unique but quite practical. The living room is sunken two short steps below the main level. The large entrance foyer channels traffic to all areas of the house. The open planned family room-kitchen area features a wood-burning fireplace. The housewife has a wonderful work area behind the kitchen which includes the laundry equipment, storage closets and a bath with shower. Maximum privacy is afforded the large patio area since it is enclosed on three sides. No. 9818.

AREA	SQ. FT.
First floor	—2,076
Basement	— 774
Garage	— 504

Arroyo

Brick, diamond windows blend perfectly

This well designed French Provincial design is a beautiful home. The brick, diamond windows, cupola, shutters, and color scheme all blend together perfectly. The floor plan is equally desirable. The three bedrooms are served by two full baths and there is a half-bath combined with the laundry, next to the family room. Sliding glass doors in the family room open onto a patio at the rear. No. 9360.

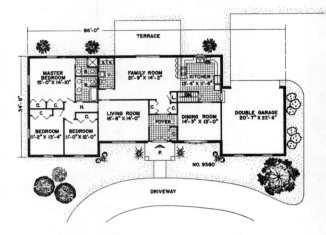

AREA	SQ. FT.
First floor	—2,055
Basement	—2,063
Garage	— 517

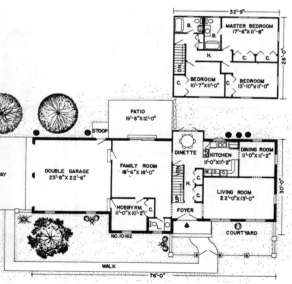

Harrington

Courtyard prelude to unique design

Fenced with ornamental iron railings, the airy courtyard becomes an appropriate prelude to this traditionally styled home. Brick, stucco, and half timber siding combine with red cedar shingles and small-paned windows to create a delightful facade. Inside, the emphasis is on space, and the floor plan is highlighted by large living and family rooms, a closeted hobby room, half bath, formal dining room, kitchen, and breakfast room. For outdoor living, a roomy patio annexes the family room via sliding glass doors. No. 10162.

AREA	SQ. FT.
First floor	—1,451
Second floor	— 853
Basement	—1,434
Garage	— 586

Ancaster

Exceptional exterior previews plan

Luxury and fine detailing apparent in the shake-shingled hipped roof, stone siding and bow window of this traditional design are programmed into the floor plan as well. To the left of the foyer, a formal living room and dining room announce their presence with dignity derived from the graceful bow window. Informality reigns in the generous family room, which merits a fireplace and access to the terrace, where a vented barbecue grill suggests the pleasures of outdoor dining. Three and one half baths are featured. No. 9854.

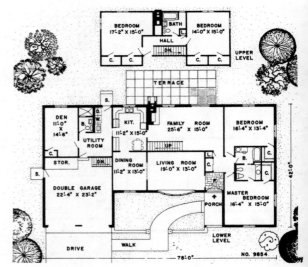

AREA	SQ. FT.
First floor	—2,268
Second floor	— 781
Basement	—1,125
Garage	— 576

Collins

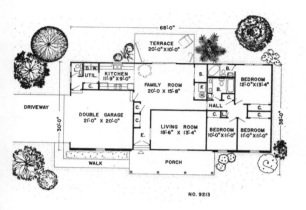

NO. 9213

This beautiful home has many desirable features such as no cross traffic through the living room, privacy in the bedroom area and maximum convenience in the kitchen area. The plan is shown without a basement but a stairway can be built into the storage and furnace room area if a basement is desired. The family room is extra large and opens onto the terrace through sliding glass doors. The garage doors can be installed in front if necessary. No. 9213.

AREA	SQ. FT.
First floor	—1,615
Garage	— 443

Destry

Main living area forms octagon

With wood-burning fireplace creating a focal point, the main living area forms an octagon in this contemporary retreat. The large deck, accessible from living area and both bedrooms, assures outdoor involvement, with four pairs of sliding glass doors inviting the view. Two full baths edge the bedrooms, and a totally compact kitchen is bordered by the utility/laundry room. Designed for leisure living, this plan includes two convenient storage areas. No. 1052.

AREA	SQ. FT.
First floor	—1,060
Outside storage	— 48
Carport	— 360

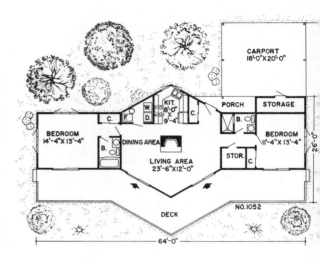

Chapman

Contemporary elects exceptional exterior

Two vaulted gambrel roofs are trimmed with
a unique window treatment and cedar shakes
to fashion an attractive double-winged contemporary design. The roofs camouflage the
double garage and accent the bedroom wing,
with the master bedroom treated to an es-
calating expanse of windows. The foyer
invites entry to formal living room and provides access to informal kitchen, family
room, and patio beyond. Combination
laundry room and half bath border the family
room, and the well-placed dining room will
fill entertaining needs. No. 10210.

AREA	SQ. FT.
First floor	—2,182
Basement	—2,182
Garage	— 480

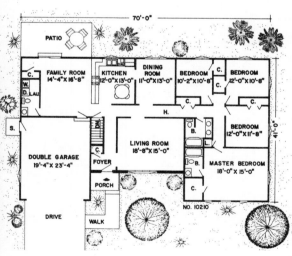

Royce

A home with a court yard offers many advantages, especially in an urban area. Outdoor living can be enjoyed in complete privacy. Also, an abundance of natural light can be utilized, again with maximum privacy. This house was designed for an active family that likes to entertain. A teenage party can take place in the rumpus room without disturbing an adult gathering in the family room. Two full baths, plenty of closets and a double garage complete the picture to provide an excellent floor plan. No. 9265.

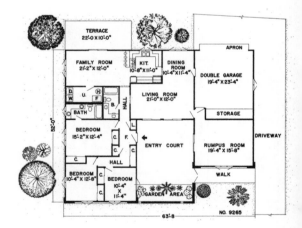

AREA	SQ. FT.
First floor	—2,047
Garage	— 473

Shawano

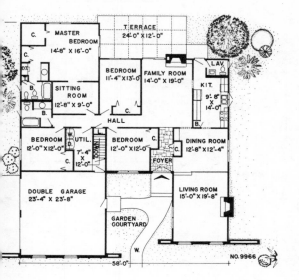

Superb bedroom suite shares terrace

Distinctive in this Spanish masterpiece is the picturesque master bedroom suite, sketching a sizable sitting room, double closets, segmented bath and dressing area. With the fireplace-warmed family room, the master bedroom uses sliding glass doors to reach the large terrace. Three more bedrooms and a full bath are spliced with a laundry room, placed to save time and steps. The corridor kitchen is equally available to the formal dining room and family room and is bordered by a half bath. No. 9966.

AREA	SQ. FT.
First floor	—2,396
Basement	—2,396
Garage	— 576

Placid

Up-to-date plan embraces tradition

Besides its appealing shuttered exterior, this one and one half story traditional also reflects the charm of the past in its floor plan. Entry reveals a formal dining room at left, dead-end living room at right, and straight ahead, a gracious stairway to the upper level. To meet contemporary needs, the hallway leads to a cozy firelit family room, open to the patio via sliding glass doors. The first floor master bedroom merits its own bath and can also serve as a convenient guest room. No. 10286.

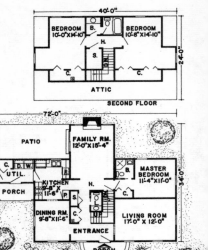

AREA	SQ. FT.
First floor	—1,157
Second floor	— 652
Basement	—1,087
Garage	— 440

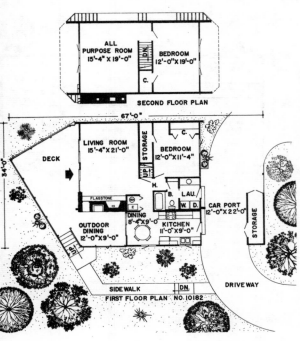

Millwright

Outdoor dining slated for deck

Dining in the fresh air is encouraged by the 12-foot outdoor dining room, equipped with built-in barbecue grill, and part of the massive deck area in this rustic leisure plan. Two pairs of sliding glass doors separate the deck from the substantial living room, highlighted by wood-burning fireplace. Ample storage space serves the first floor bedroom, which is bordered by full bath and laundry. Upstairs, another large bedroom and an all purpose room promise sleeping quarters for family and visiting friends. No. 10182.

AREA	SQ. FT.
First floor	—968
Second floor	—640
Carport	—264

Manorfield

Barbecue Encourages Outdoor Living

Entrance to this home is gained through a large foyer opening to a central hall. The large versatile living room/dining room area is centrally located between the kitchen and family room for maximum usage. Incorporated into the kitchen, itself, is a breakfast area suitable for most of a busy family's meals. No. 348.

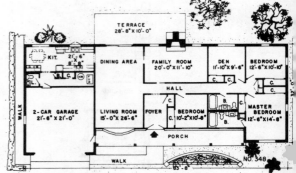

AREA	SQ. FT.
First floor	—2,094
Garage	— 492

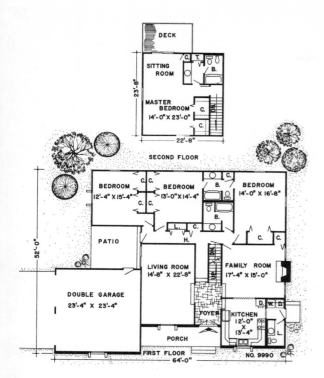

Sporatan

Bedroom Masters Inside, Outside

Dominating the exterior of this gracious brick-layered design, the master bedroom suite heightens the interior as well, offering a sitting room, double walk-in closets, luxurious bath, and sliding glass doors to private deck. Not to be outdone, three more bedrooms are lavish, sharing two full baths and bountiful closets. Formal and informal areas are defined by the entrance foyer, which allows access to sunken living room, family room and kitchen. Enclosed on three sides, a patio is open to living room and bedroom hallway. No. 9990.

AREA	SQ. FT.
First floor	—2,113
Second floor	— 538
Basement	—2,113
Garage	— 576

Medford

Studio strengthens Dutch colonial

Reminiscent of a Dutch colonial farmhouse, this massive triple-sectioned design is heightened by a serviceable studio or game room above garage. Emphasizing privacy, the design groups three bedrooms and two baths in second floor sleeping wing and further separates the master bedroom by closets, bath and stairway. Sliding glass doors open the family room and firelit living room to terraces, and a dining room is set apart to stress formality. Bordering the kitchen is a combination laundry and half bath. No. 10016.

AREA	SQ. FT.
First floor	—1,256
Second floor	— 815
Garage	— 576
Garage—2nd	— 384
Basement	— 936

Alamosa

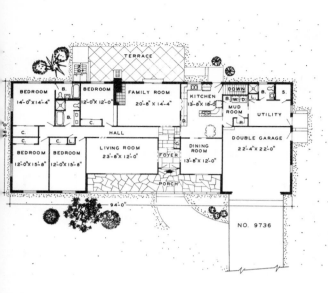

Mud room doubles as laundry center

Separating garage and kitchen, the mud room of this stone-sheathed ranch style doubles as laundry center, freeing the utility room for use as workshop or sewing room. Careful detailing is apparent throughout the plan, which creates an efficient kitchen with dining space, planning desk, and pass-through to the family room. Corner fireplace and terrace benefit the family room, while living and dining room retain formality. Sleeping wing provides four bedrooms, including a master bedroom with private bath as well as a compartmented family bath with both tub and shower. No. 9736.

AREA	SQ. FT.
First floor	—2,725
Basement	—2,725
Garage	— 547

Vickshire

Distinctive Colonial is split-level design

A roofed outdoor living area, balcony and curved inner stairway combine to make this colonial a gracious split-level. The slate foyer directs traffic to the three bedrooms and two baths, down to the basement, or up a few steps to the family room, kitchen and living area. The family room, with a wood-burning fireplace in one corner, opens to a balcony which leads to the roofed outdoor area. The kitchen is open to the family room, with a folding door providing privacy when needed. The 15' x 13' master bedroom is served by its own bath. No. 9772.

AREA	SQ. FT.
First floor	—1,846
Basement	—1,846
Garage	— 521

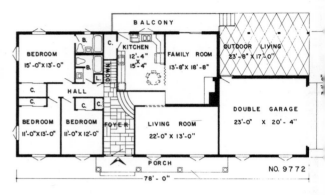

"J·R·BRESLER"

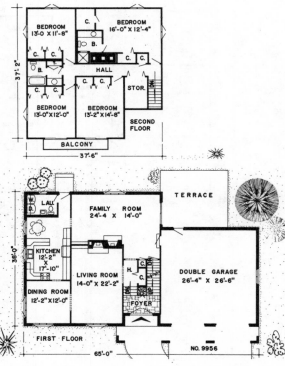

Spanada

Dramatic arches encompass home

Carefully placed arches camouflage the garage and accent the windows in this Spanish design. The inviting effect is continued in the gracious tiled foyer, which allows access to both floors. Down three steps are the living room and family room, both favored with wood-burning fireplaces. No. 9956.

AREA	SQ. FT.
First floor	—1,414
Second floor	—1,310
Basement	—1,414
Garage	— 756

Brandon

Living room highlights ranch style

Dramatically punctuated by a wood-burning fireplace on one end and glass access to the terrace on the other, the expansive living room becomes the focus of this distinctive ranch style. Two closets furnish the long foyer, and, to the right, three bedrooms and two full baths are nestled in the sleeping wing. Behind the double garage, the utility complex merits a laundry center and full bath with shower, while the large kitchen offers informal dining space. No. 10176.

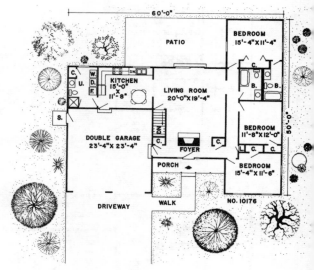

AREA	SQ. FT.
First floor	—1,608
Basement	—1,608
Garage	— 576

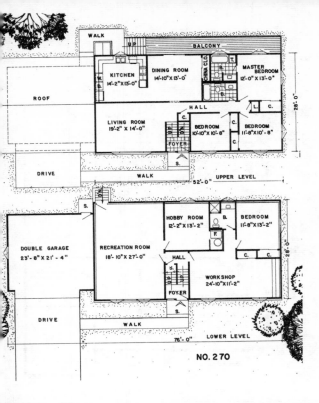

WALK
UP
BALCONY
ROOF
KITCHEN
14'-2" X 13'-0"
DINING ROOM
14'-10" X 13'-0"
CHINA CLO.
B.
T.
MASTER
BEDROOM
12'-0" X 13'-0"
28'-0"
HALL
LIVING ROOM
19'-2" X 14'-0"
C.
BEDROOM
10'-10" X 10'-8"
C.
BEDROOM
11'-8" X 10'-8"
C.
FOYER
DRIVE
WALK
52'-0"   UPPER LEVEL
S.

S.
HOBBY ROOM
12'-2" X 13'-2"
B.
BEDROOM
11'-8" X 13'-2"
28'-0"
DOUBLE GARAGE
23'-8" X 21'-4"
RECREATION ROOM
18'-10" X 27'-0"
HALL
C.
C.
WORKSHOP
24'-10" X 11'-2"
FOYER
S.
DRIVE
WALK
76'-0"   LOWER LEVEL

NO. 270

Mattoon

Family living for the budget minded . . .

Two story efficiency and one story economy are combined to produce this roomy split foyer design. The rectangular shape assures minimum costs for maximum liveable area. A large family can live peacefully in this home without stumbling over each other. The balcony at the rear, while not absolutely essential, provides an outdoor area for sun bathing or just relaxing to enjoy a cool evening breeze. The large garage provides storage space for bicycles, the lawn mower, etc. No. 270.

AREA	SQ. FT.
Upper level	—1,456
Lower level	—1,456
Garage	— 528

Devonport

The home of a lifetime . . . offering an outstanding plan that's unique in every way!

Distinctive as this home may appear, with its deck-encircled hexagonal living room, its construction will actually prove practical. Besides the living room, which exhibits exposed beams and a cathedral ceiling, the main level encompasses four bedrooms, two baths, dining room and kitchen. On the lower level, an enormous family room opens to a patio, with built-in barbecue. Another bedroom, den and bath with shower are detailed. Boat storage is also provided on this level No. 9950.

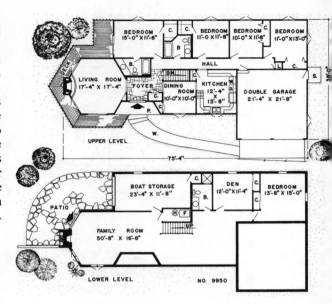

AREA	SQ. FT.
First floor	—1,672
Lower level	—1,672
Garage	— 484

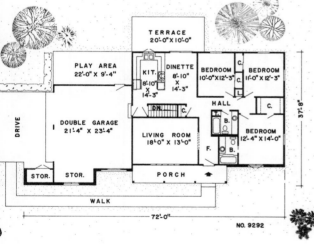

Hampshire

Terrace, play area border kitchen

Assuming a quiet dignity with its stone and antique brick exterior, this moderate size design was created with small children and outdoor relaxation in mind. Fringing the kitchen is a sizable play area and a terrace which connects to the dining area via sliding glass doors. Three adequate bedrooms are provided, including a master bedroom with full bath and walk-in closet. Storage is incorporated in the double garage, and a full basement is featured. No. 9292.

AREA	SQ. FT.
First floor	—1,366
Garage and storage	— 619
Basement	—1,366

Skyline

Circular stairs, sun deck enrich design

Inspired by the French Riviera, this massive design incorporates several striking features, including a circular stairway leading to an extensive sun deck over the garage. Wood-burning fireplaces are enjoyed by both the sunken living room and the lavish master bedroom suite. Three more sizable bedrooms and a functional bath comprise the upper level. The formal dining room is bordered by a spacious kitchen with dining space, and a convenient laundry room and half bath complete the hallway. No. 9976.

AREA	SQ. FT.
First floor	—1,290
Second floor	—1,277
Basement	— 992
Garage	— 535

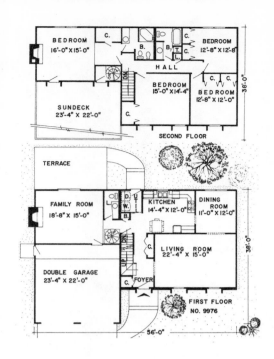

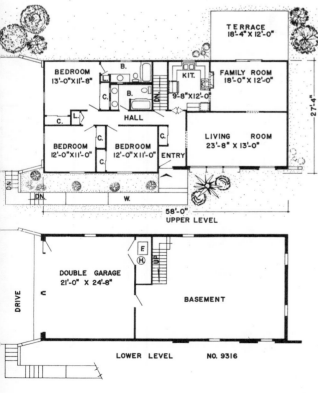

Floor plan labels:

TERRACE 18'-4" X 12'-0"

BEDROOM 13'-0"X11'-8"

B.

KIT.

FAMILY ROOM 18'-0" X 12'-0"

9'-8"X12'-0"

C.

L.

HALL

DN.

27'-4"

C.

BEDROOM 12'-0"X11'-0"

C.

BEDROOM 12'-0"X11'-0"

C.

LIVING ROOM 23'-8" X 13'-0"

ENTRY

DN.

DN.

W.

58'-0"

UPPER LEVEL

DRIVE

DOUBLE GARAGE 21'-0" X 24'-8"

E
H

UP

BASEMENT

LOWER LEVEL   NO. 9316

Finsbury

Center hallway channels traffic

Immediate access to the living room, kitchen, and bedroom wing is made possible by the centrally placed entrance hall in this brick-trimmed Mediterranean design. Bordered by the kitchen and living room, the family room annexes the concrete terrace via sliding glass doors. The sleeping wing features three well-closeted bedrooms, a bath and linen closet private to the master bedroom, and a hall bath with double sinks. A full basement including a double garage is indicated. No. 9316.

AREA	SQ. FT.
First floor	—1,548
Garage and basement	—1,508

Westmore

Airy atmosphere pervades split level

Down three steps from the gracious foyer, the main level of this well-ordered split level breathes with light and space. The lavish array of windows brightens the living room and recreation room beneath, both of which are endowed with wood-burning fireplaces. The master bedroom is enriched with its own full bath and built-in dressing table and towel closet, while the main bathroom encompasses both tub and shower. An open air porch is reached via sliding glass doors from the living room and dining room. No. 9048.

AREA	SQ. FT.
First floor	—1,763
Basement	—1,763
Garage	— 459

Dunbar

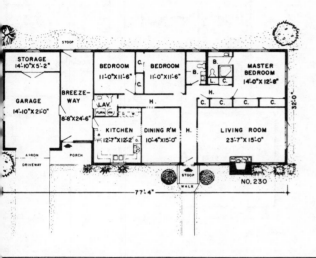

Enclosed Breezway Supplies Play Area

Completely enclosed and comfortably heated, the long breezway in this brick-encased ranch style opens to kitchen and provides an ideal play area or family room. Sleeping areas to the rear of the plan are indulged with closet space, while living area proportions generous rooms, including a 23 foot living room with fireplace. The U-shaped kitchen etches a laundry center, concealable with folding doors, and borders a formal dining room. An oversize garage allots storage space, and a half bath adjoins the breezeway. No. 230.

AREA	SQ. FT.
First floor	—1,686
Breezeway	— 229
Garage	— 448

DeLand

Living room encourages entertaining

Radiating all the charm and welcome of a French country home, this four bedroom design is highlighted by a generously pro-portioned living room with fireplace. Its sliding glass doors connect to the terrace and permit open, enjoyable entertaining. A formal dining room and kitchen with laundry space border the living room and the set-off family room. The master bedroom enjoys a bath and huge closet, while three more bedrooms and another bath are outlined. No. 9846.

AREA	SQ. FT.
First floor	—2,022
Basement	—2,022
Garage	— 576

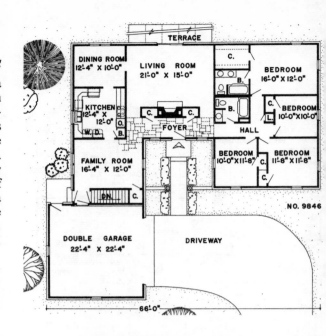

Chandler

Wooden decks are nice for summer dining

Variegated brick, rich wood siding, and diamond light windows layer the exterior of this split foyer plan. Inside, four bedrooms and a den, plus a large recreation room provide space for privacy and relaxation. Besides the recreation room, a den, bedroom, utility room and bath are found on the lower level. Upstairs, the comfortable living room enjoys a fireplace, and the dining room includes sliding glass doors to the elevated wooden deck, a natural setting for summer dining. No. 9308.

AREA	SQ. FT.
Upper level	—1,440
Lower level	—1,344
Garage	— 297

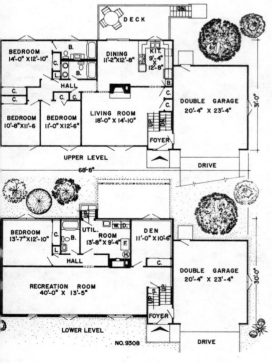

Almonte

This beautiful traditionally styled French Provincial design is planned for a modern family. Texture is emphasized on the exterior by using a cedar shake shingle roof, used brick and board and batten siding. The floor plan is exceptionally well planned, featuring three bedrooms with large closets. The living room is isolated from all cross traffic, allowing a formal atmosphere to be maintained. The two bathrooms are centrally located for maximum efficiency. The garage doors are shown on the side to improve the appearance of the front elevation. Sliding glass doors in the kitchen lead to the outdoor dining area which is entirely under one roof. No. 9684.

AREA	SQ. FT.
First Floor	—1,313
Basement	—1,313
Garage	— 482

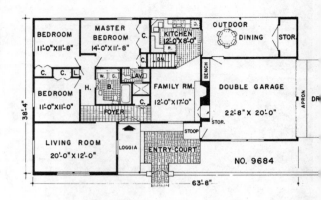

Valdosta

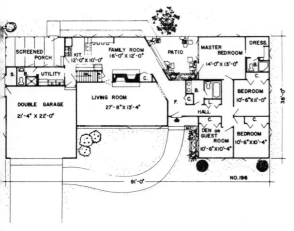

This beautiful contemporary design has just about everything an active, growing family could desire. The bedroom area contains four bedrooms and two full baths. The closets are large and the circulation between rooms is excellent. The living room is extra large and has many furniture arrangement possibilities. Open planning is featured in the kitchen-family room area and contains a built-in breakfast counter, wood-burning fireplace and sliding glass doors which open onto the covered patio. The screened porch will make an excellent outdoor, insect-free dining room. The bathroom behind the garage contains a shower. It is convenient to both the kitchen and the outdoors. No. 196.

AREA	SQ. FT.
First floor	—1,805
Basement	— 970
Garage	— 475

Capetown

Small Plan Comfortable, Individual

Efficient utilization of space is accomplished with 1194 square feet of living area in this engaging design. Two bedrooms plus a den, sizable enough to serve as a third bedroom, use two large baths, one private to the master bedroom. A spacious living room opens to the terrace, which has access to the storage area behind the garage. Open planning creates an illusion of space in the dining room and kitchen area, carefully planned to include laundry and storage areas. No. 236.

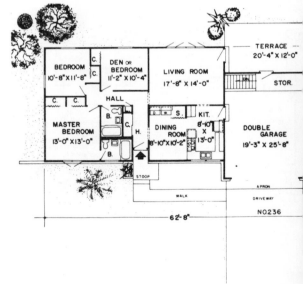

AREA	SQ. FT.
First floor	—1,194
Basement	—1,194
Garage	— 521

Madison

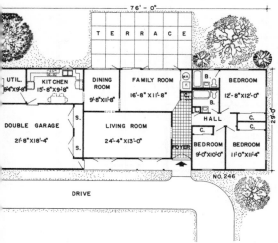

Ranch Issues Invitation to Outdoors

Shaping a sleek silhouette, this rustic ranch style calls forth images of forests and wildlife and encourages enjoyment of the outdoors. An immense terrace is open to the family room through sliding glass doors, and a formal dining room is placed to take advantage of the view. Tall, shuttered windows light the impressive living room, and a comfortable master bedroom appendages a full bath. A sizable kitchen with breakfast area has ready access to the double garage and borders a laundry/utility room. No. 246.

AREA	SQ. FT.
First floor	—1,642
Garage	— 462

Maywood

Interior offers agreeable surprises

Despite its rather compact appearance, this well-proportioned split level incorporates some unexpected conveniences. Plans call for a master bedroom with bountiful closet space and private bath with shower, in addition to the full bath which serves the two smaller bedrooms. A 20 foot family room is shown on the lower level and borders a spacious laundry and utility room. The sizable living room and dining area are equally accessible to the kitchen. No. 166.

AREA	SQ. FT.
Living area	—1,088
Family room	— 543

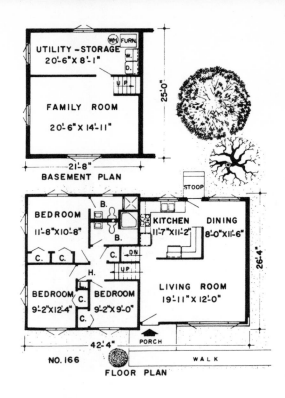

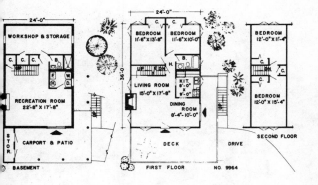

Neuchatel

Recreation room houses fireplace

Restful log fires will contribute atmosphere to the sizable recreation room bounding the patio of this chalet. Upstairs, another fireplace warms the living and dining rooms which are accessible to the large wooden sun deck. Four bedrooms and two baths are outlined, and the home is completely insulated for year round convenience. No. 9964.

AREA	SQ. FT.
First floor	—896
Second floor	—457
Basement	—864

Cortez

Spanish styling inspires ranch plan

Triple arches and ornamented railing deck this Spanish ranch, filled with intricate touches of luxury. Stretching over 26 feet, the master bedroom suite chooses full bath, double closets and double entrances, and might be partitioned to form another bedroom. Log-burning fireplaces warming living room and family room help buffer noise, and double sliding glass doors open family room to terrace. Edging the kitchen, a dinette opens to the patio, and a formal dining room is also provided. No. 10022.

AREA	SQ. FT.
First floor	—2,552
Basement	—2,552
Garage	— 576

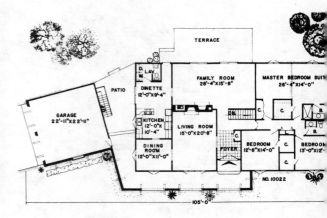

Shoreham

Fireplace inspires romantic dining

Pleasurable dining in the expansive living-dining area is created by the atmospheric wood-burning fireplace in this brick-layered traditional. A functional breakfast bar joins the kitchen and family room, which is placed to enjoy the terrace. A gracious foyer eliminates cross-traffic and allows access to the living or sleeping wing, where three sizable bedrooms and two full baths are provided. The double garage also opens to the terrace. No. 9908.

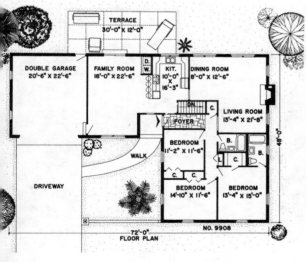

AREA	SQ. FT.
First floor	1,896
Basement	—1,896
Garage	— 509

Midland

Three Bedrooms Option in Plan

Two bedrooms can be constructed in the future at the front of this attractive ranch style. Meanwhile, the large master bedroom enjoys a walk-in closet and private bath, with a second bath ready for guests. A firelit living room merits sliding glass doors to the terrace, and the narrow, efficient kitchen is flanked by laundry and dining room. No. 358.

AREA	SQ. FT.
Living Area	—1,395
Front Bedrooms	— 288

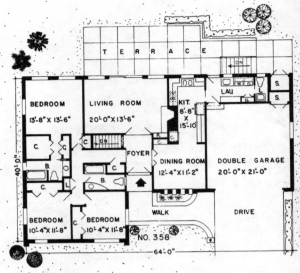

Sidney

Vacation retreat enjoyable all year

Fully insulated ceilings and outside walls and first class construction will assure a leisure home that can be enjoyed throughout the year in this space-conserving two bedroom plan. On the lower level, a full bath with shower adjoins the laundry/utility room, and garage and boat storage are provided. Simple but efficient, the upstairs floor plan outlines two closeted bedrooms and full bath with linen closet. The kitchen is open to the spacious living/dining area, and sliding glass doors open to the deck for sunbathing or savoring the view. No. 10170.

AREA	SQ. FT.
Upper level	—860
Lower level	—836

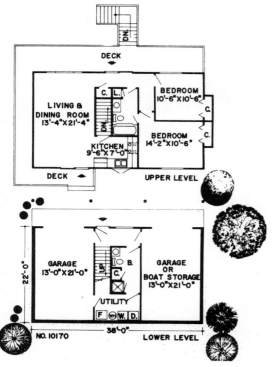

DECK

LIVING & DINING ROOM 13'-4"x21'-4"

C. L.

BEDROOM 10'-6"x10'-6"

C.

KITCHEN 9'-6"x7'-0"

BEDROOM 14'-2"x10'-6"

C.

DECK

UPPER LEVEL

GARAGE 13'-0"x21'-0"

B.

C.

GARAGE OR BOAT STORAGE 13'-0"x21'-0"

UTILITY

F W. D.

NO. 10170

22'-0"

38'-0"

LOWER LEVEL

Berkely

Simplicity, comfort focuses of home

Maximum economy and livability is accomplished simultaneously in this attractive brick trimmed ranch design. Shuttered windows and a gable roof create an appealing exterior, while the interior outlines a workable floor plan featuring three bedrooms and two full baths. The living room is ample, and the kitchen is assigned a handy breakfast bar. A separate dining room features sliding glass doors opening to the terrace. Another advantage is the full basement, accessible from the kitchen via an open stairway. No. 158.

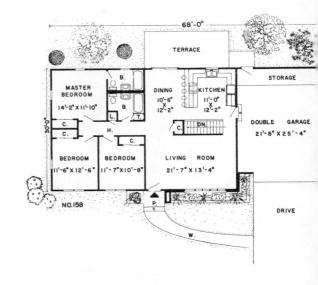

AREA	SQ. FT.
First floor	—1,380
Basement	—1,380
Garage	— 572

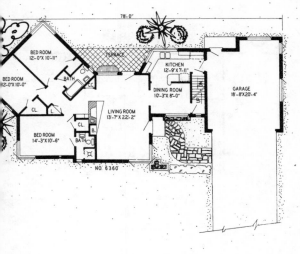

Fernridge

Ranch style favors living room

Stretching over 22 feet to span the width of this ranch design, the living room is indulged with expanses of windows, wood-burning fireplace, and access to the terrace. Separate, well-windowed dining room and efficient kitchen with abundant counter space border the living room. No. 6360.

AREA	SQ. FT.
House	—1,293
Basement	— 767
Garage	— 466
Terrace	— 92

Durham

Kitchen complex useful, adaptable

Bordered by dining room on one side and dinette and utility room on the other, the kitchen takes command of a highly useful complex in this three bedroom design. Should the dinette not be needed for eating space, it might adapt to a sewing, hobby, or play room. Fireplace and picture window brighten the 22 foot living room, and the master bedroom enjoys an excellent closet and full bath. Another full bath is placed to serve bedrooms and living areas. No. 8266.

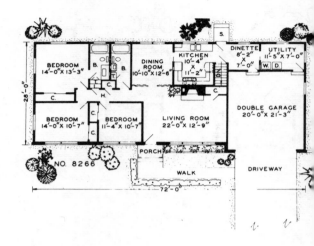

AREA	SQ. FT.
First floor	—1,604
Garage	— 455
Basement	—1,604

Ardan

Living-dining room focus of plan

Sunlight glistening through diamond light windows, glowing wood-burning fireplace, and annexed sun deck combine to fashion a living-dining room that sparkles with personality. Separated from the dining area by sliding glass doors, the sizable deck offers eating space outdoors, while the breakfast bar invites quick snacks in the kitchen. Fireplace-dominated recreation room shares lower level with hobby room, bedroom, and bath, and master bedroom is enriched with double closets and private bath. No. 9312.

AREA	SQ. FT.
Upper level	—1,549
Lower level	—1,500
Garage	— 528

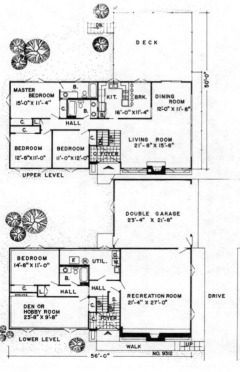

Chartrand

Balcony enriches facade, bedrooms

Two bedrooms enjoy a bonus in the 23-foot balcony that fronts this split level plan. Stone veneer, ornamental iron railings, and French doors create an eye-catching exterior, while effective zoning distinguishes the interior. Living areas are cozy and include firelit living room, well-proportioned dining room open to the terrace. No. 10128.

AREA	SQ. FT.
Living levels	—1,344
Garage levels	— 720

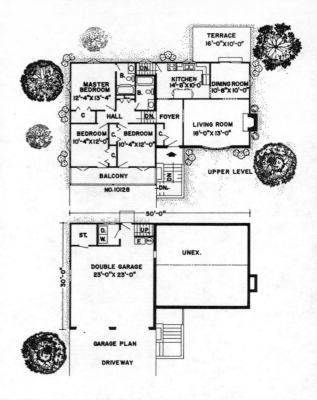

Chaffee

Enclosed porch lengthens family room

Airy and restful, an enclosed porch opens to the family room in this moderate split level and sets the scene for outdoor entertaining and relaxation. Contrasting horizontal and vertical siding blend with brick to complete a lovely exterior; inside, the floor plan is efficient. Eating space is apportioned in the sizable kitchen, which serves both family room and living room. Three closeted bedrooms, include master bedroom with full bath, and another half bath border the lower level laundry and storage area. No. 164.

AREA	SQ. FT.
Living areas	—1,345
Garage level	— 608

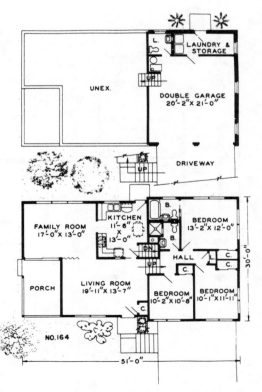

LAUNDRY & STORAGE

UNEX.

DOUBLE GARAGE
20'-2" X 21'-0"

DRIVEWAY

KITCHEN
11'-6"
X
13'-0"

BEDROOM
13'-2" X 12'-0"

FAMILY ROOM
17'-0" X 13'-0"

HALL

PORCH

LIVING ROOM
19'-11" X 13'-7"

BEDROOM
10'-2" X 10'-8"

BEDROOM
10'-1" X 11'-11"

NO.164

51'-0"

30'-0"

Millington

Colonial ranch style, enriched interior

Endowed with the trimmings of a traditional colonial, this three bedroom ranch style becomes doubly attractive with the addition of modern features. For example, the sizable master bedroom annexes a full bath with shower, walk-in closet and spacious dressing area. Warmed by a wood-burning fireplace, the living room spills onto a large redwood deck via sliding glass doors. A functional kitchen is separated from the family room by a cooking peninsula, and a utility room and hobby shop edge the double garage. No. 9864.

AREA	SQ. FT.
First floor	—1,612
Basement	—1,612
Garage, utility and storage	— 660

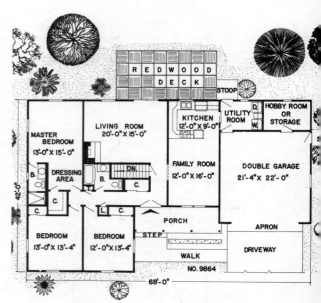

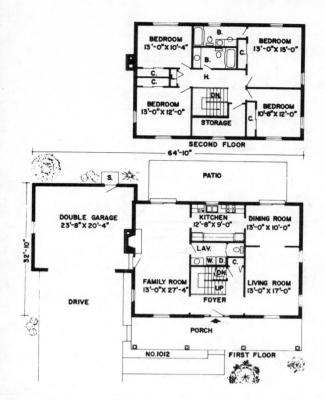

Biloxi

Facade repeats rich southern tradition

Repeating the gracious charm of traditional Southern Colonial homes, the engaging exterior of this four bedroom design displays two story columns and a sweeping front porch. Inside, rooms are large and livable, with a 27-foot family room sporting fireplace and sliding glass doors to the terrace. The corridor kitchen is well-placed, serving both family room and formal dining room, and the living room borders the foyer. Four bedrooms, two baths, and an ample storage area make up the second story. No. 1012.

AREA	SQ. FT.
First floor	—1,177
Second floor	—1,177
Basement	—1,177
Garage	— 542

Bakersfield

The popularity of split foyer designs continues to grow. One reason is that they not only maintain their resale value but usually the value appreciates considerably. This one has a very attractive facade which includes a large bow window in the living room and two square bay windows in the front bedrooms. The living-dining room area is quite large and offers a large amount of furniture arrangement possibilities. The lower level recreation room provides plenty of space for parties and family activities. No. 9310.

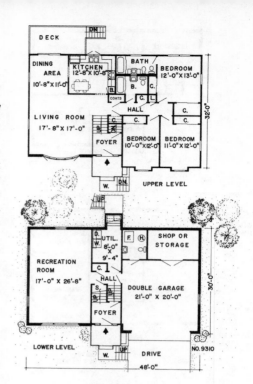

AREA	SQ. FT.
Upper level	—1,461
Lower level	— 740
Garage and shop	— 651

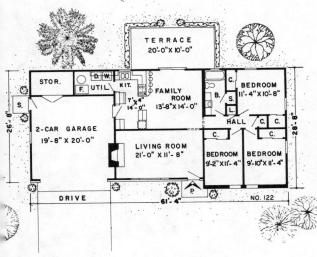

Donovan

Open planning benefits family room

Informality and serviceability result from the use of open planning in the kitchen-family room area of this dignified three bedroom design. A useful breakfast bar separates the two rooms, and the family room opens to the terrace via sliding glass doors. More formality is possible in the large living room, brightened by excellent window treatment and a wood-burning fireplace. Three bedrooms with ample closet space are provided, and a large storage area is indicated behind the garage. No. 122.

AREA	SQ. FT.
First floor	—1,204
Garage	— 406
Storage	— 65

Vienne

French design carried through interior

The formality of this French country home is preserved in its interior planning. Four bedrooms, including a master bedroom with wood-burning fireplace, completes the upstairs. The lower level contains breakfast nook, utility room, formal dining room, kitchen, family and living rooms and a den or library. The spacious kitchen includes a built-in range and oven, a planning nook and breakfast bar. The formal living room is free of all cross traffic. Two full and two half-baths complete the plan. No. 9878.

AREA	SQ. FT.
First floor	—1,759
Second floor	— 972
Basement	—1,496
Garage	— 590

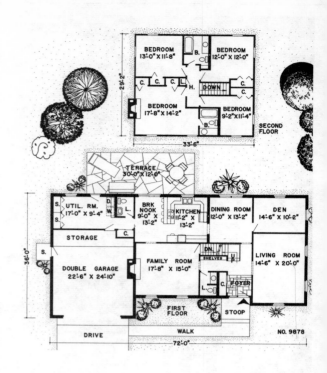

MacVicar

Half timber, stucco layer design

Reminiscent of the English Tudor architecture popular years ago, this half timber and stucco plan greets its new popularity with a floor plan that caters to modern needs. In the living room, a wood-burning fireplace gives the interior a rustic charm of its own. The kitchen borders a useful half-bath and laundry on one side and dining room on the other. Three bedrooms and two full baths occupy the upper level. No. 10100.

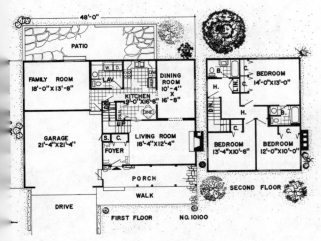

AREA	SQ. FT.
First floor	—1,089
Second floor	— 792
Basement	—1,089
Garage	— 484

Vidalia

Master bedroom merits private patio

Impressive and enticing, the master bedroom suite sets the tone of studied luxury in this traditional design. The suite features a private patio, two large closets and and a deluxe bath, as well as an entrance to the adjoining nursery or den. Two more bedrooms and a bath complete the wing, and a maid's room or hobby room with bath is situated behind the garage. Fireplaces warm both the living room and family room, which has access to the terrace. No. 9906.

AREA	SQ. FT.
First floor	—2,492
Basement	—2,492
Garage	— 552

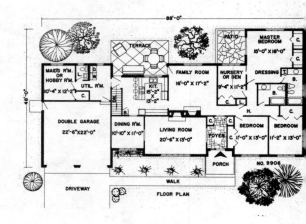

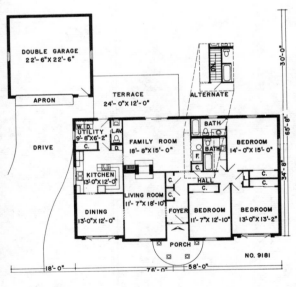

Willmar

Roofed walkway attaches garage

Placed behind the home and separate, so as not to detract from the rich traditional facade, the garage in this Colonial plan is attached by a roofed walkway. Brick and white pillars grace the exterior, while the interior floor plan speaks of modern luxury. Formal living room and dining room are placed to the left of the foyer. No. 9181.

AREA	SQ. FT.
First floor	—2,014
Garage	— 576

Sagamore

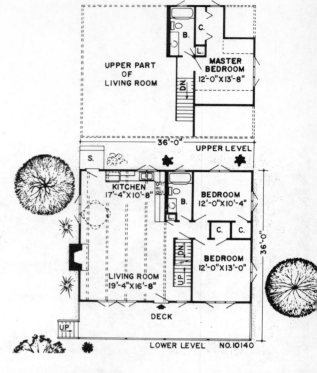

Rustic exterior; complete home

Rustic though it is in appearance, the interior of this cabin is quiet, modern and comfortable. Small in overall size, it still contains three bedrooms and two baths in addition to a large, two story living room with exposed beams. As a hunting or fishing lodge or a mountain retreat, this compares well. No. 10140.

AREA	SQ. FT.
First floor	—1,008
Second floor	— 281
Basement	—1,008

Durango

Distinctive ranch masters convenience

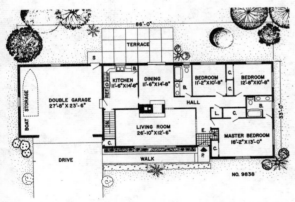

Carefully designed and trimmed in brick, this attractive ranch style displays a floor plan that emphasizes convenience. The tiled foyer allows access to both living and sleeping areas, and the double garage is elongated to provide boat storage area. A striking two-way fireplace adds drama to both living room and dining room, and a plush master bedroom suite furnishes two closets and a spacious bath with built-in vanity and double sinks. No. 9838.

AREA	SQ. FT.
First floor	—1,770
Basement	—1,770
Garage	— 700

Prescott

Come on in, the living's fine . . .

This house leaves little to be desired in a comfortable family home. A few of the most outstanding features are a private patio off of the master bedroom; a two-way fireplace between the living room and family room; a built-in charcoal grill in the family room; a bath with shower next to the kitchen and handy to the pool area and a very nice breakfast nook with a view of the pool area. The mud room is large enough to serve as a sewing and ironing room as well as the laundry. The low maintenance exterior of beautiful natural stone blends well with the shake shingle roof. No. 9828.

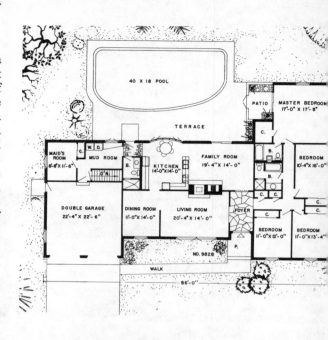

AREA	SQ. FT.
First floor	—2,679
Basement	—2,679
Garage	— 541

Boswell

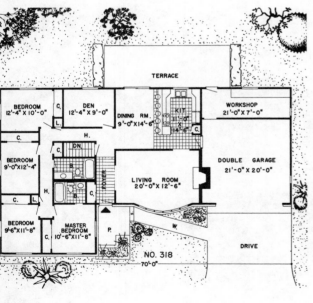

Brick jackets living room wall

Brick layers the entire wall on the fireplace end of the bow-windowed living room in this attractive home. Tiled foyer circulates traffic to living areas, sleeping areas, and basement. Divided by a long breakfast bar, kitchen and dining rooms are open and spacious, with dining room opening to terrace via sliding glass doors. Four bedrooms are indulged with closets and two tiled baths, while a den borders living areas and is adaptable to playroom or extra bedroom. Accessible to both garage and terrace, a large workshop provides both hobby space and extra storage. No. 318.

AREA	SQ. FT.
First floor	**—1,660**
Basement	**—1,660**
Garage and	
workshop	**— 596**

Prospect

Traditional exterior encloses split level

Diamond light windows, shutters, brick veneer and horizontal siding merge to create an exterior with traditional warmth and appeal in this split level plan. Living areas are substantial and include a formal living room and open dining room, supplemented by family room and huge recreation area below. In addition, lower level houses a full bath with shower and a sizable workshop. Three bedrooms are nestled on the highest level and include a 17-foot master bedroom with large private bath and double closets. No. 326.

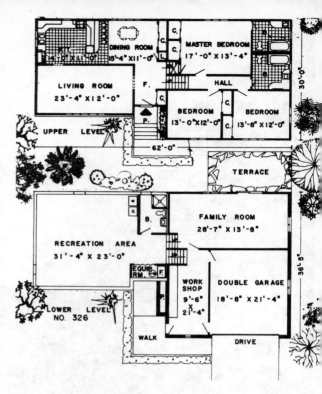

AREA	SQ. FT.
Living areas	—1,663
Garage level	—1,092
Basement	— 763

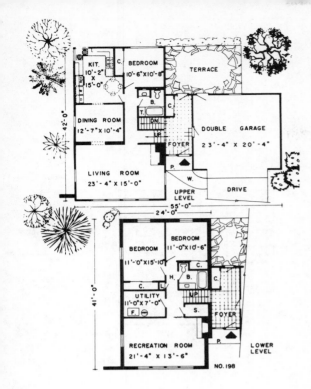

Midway

This handsome split-foyer design possesses many outstanding features. Horizontal siding, vertical siding and brick are combined to produce a very attractive exterior. The living room and the recreation room both feature woodburning fireplaces. The tiled foyer leads to both levels as well as the flagstone terrace at the rear. The kitchen is well planned and has a breakfast area. No. 198.

AREA	SQ. FT.
Upper level and foyer	—1,127
Lower level	— 975
Garage	— 504

Montclair

Vaulted ceilings effect impressive entry

Vaulted ceilings and the profusion of windows set this A-frame design alive with height and drama. The imposing living room is rendered comfortable by its wood-burning fireplace, and it adjoins the open kitchen and family room, separated by a breakfast bar. Two bedrooms with copious closet space, plus a full bath, complete the main level. The upper level houses another bedroom and bath, as well as an ample hobby room which might be furnished with a sofa bed to convert it to a guest room when necessary. A covered patio is reached through the family room. No. 9269.

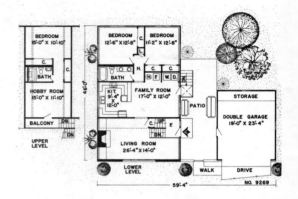

AREA	SQ. FT.
Lower level	—1,285
Upper level	— 476
Garage	— 473

Manitou

Master bedroom suite accéntuates luxury

Adorned with pillars and a bow window, this rich French Provincial design becomes an exercise in elegance, crowned by the master bedroom suite. Placed to allow full privacy, the master bedroom incorporates a segmented bath, large walk-in closet, and sitting room with its own closet. A firelit living room and dining room augment an appealing family room, which opens to the terrace. Beyond the kitchen, a laundry room, half-bath, and closet space add to the convenience. A breakfast nook with bow window overlooks the terrace. No. 9870.

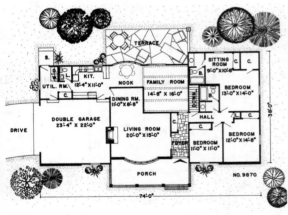

AREA	SQ. FT.
First floor	—2,015
Basement	—2,015
Garage	— 545

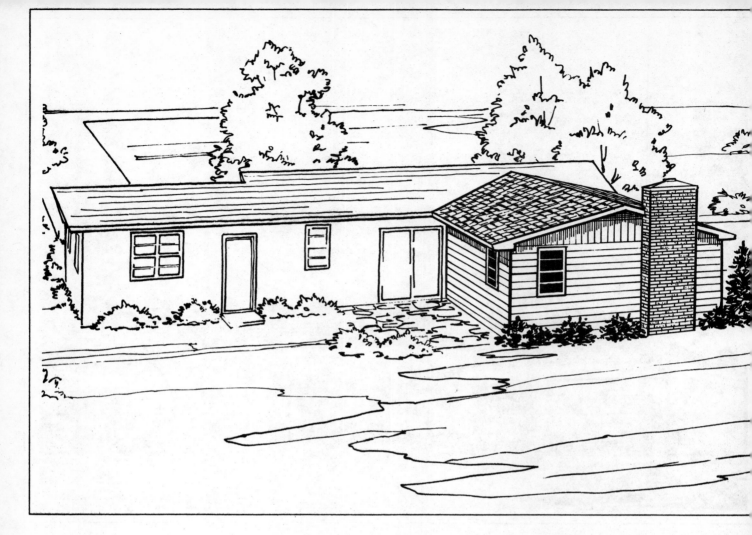

Annex One

Add a bedroom, bath, and family room

This 448-sq. ft. addition lets you relax beside a crackling fire in its 15-ft. family room, with adjoining double-closeted bedroom and full bath. No. 20010.

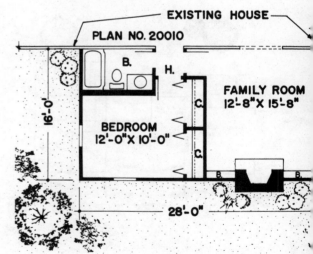

EXISTING HOUSE

PLAN NO. 20010

B.

H.

FAMILY ROOM
12'-8" X 15'-8"

16'-0"

C.

BEDROOM
12'-0" X 10'-0"

C.

B.

B.

28'-0"

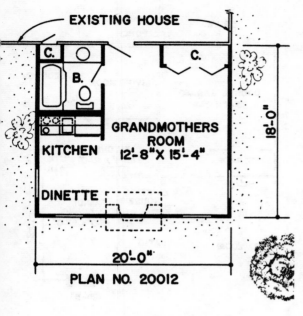

EXISTING HOUSE

C. C.

B.

GRANDMOTHERS
ROOM
12'-8" X 15'-4"

KITCHEN

DINETTE

18'-0"

20'-0"

PLAN NO. 20012

Annex Two

Annex a guest apartment

Substantial bedroom, full bath, kitchen and dinette are included in this 360-sq. ft. addition, perfect for overnight visitors or permanent guests. No. 20012.

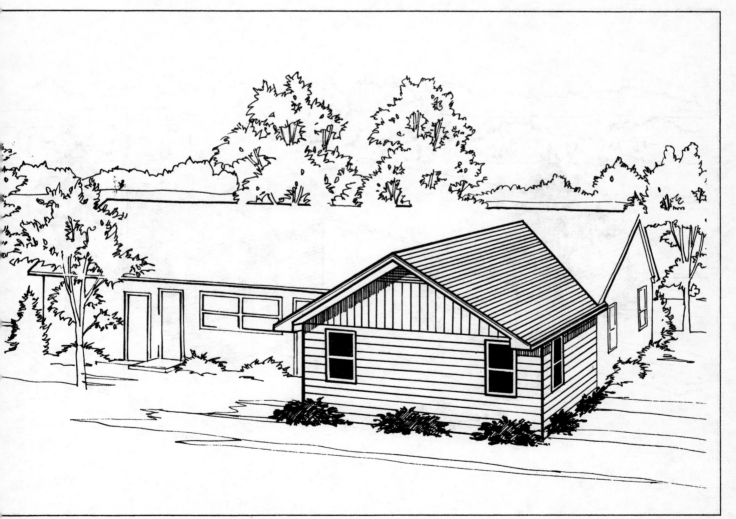

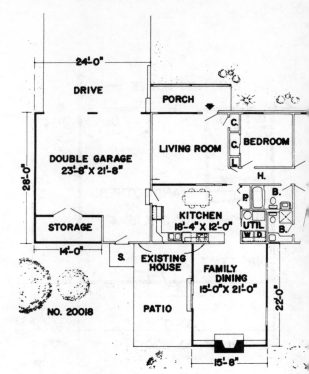

Annex Three

Attach a garage and family room

Extending from the original home in two directions are the double garage with storage and the family-dining room, a spacious living area with raised hearth fireplace, built-in bookshelves, and sliding glass doors to the patio. No. 20018.

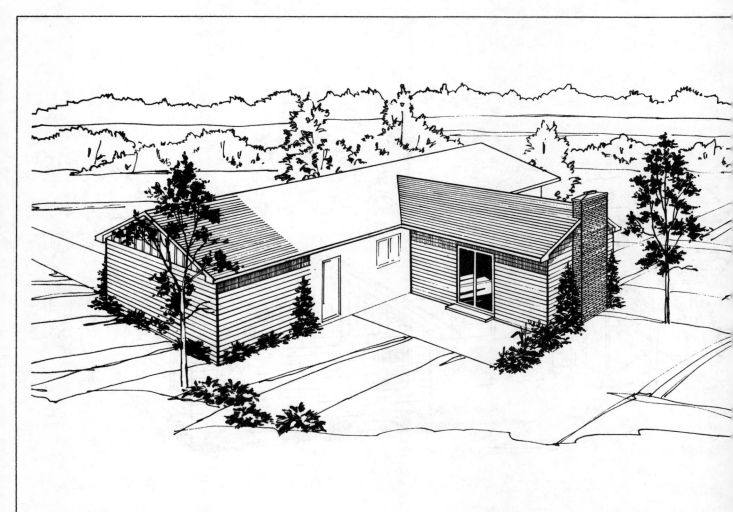

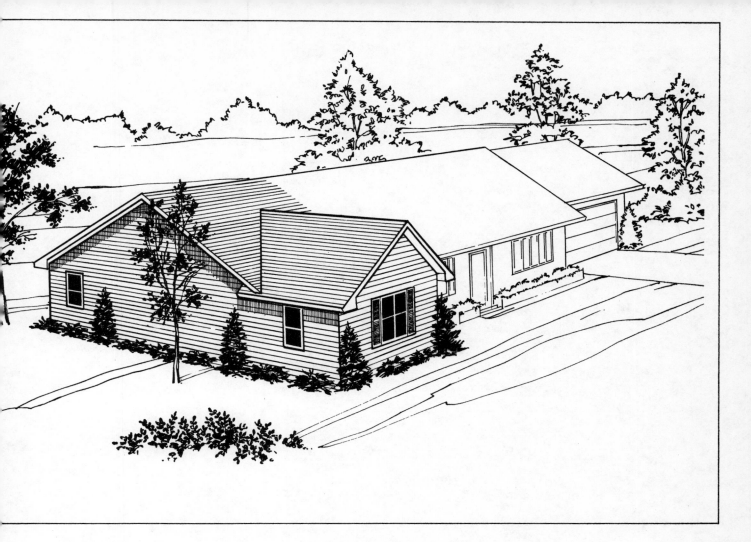

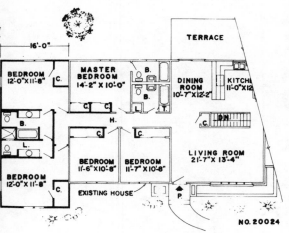

Annex Four

*Increase sleeping space
with two bedrooms, bath*

Two generously proportioned bedrooms,
each with large walk-in closets, are separated by two connecting baths in this substantial sleeping wing. No. 20024.

Index

How to Obtain Working Drawings

After selecting your favorite design, you will want to see detailed working drawings to let you compare costs on options (i.e., flooring, light fixtures, paneling, appliances). You will choose options and customize your home to suit your needs. Each set of plans includes: Four Elevations (one view of the home from each of the four sides showing slope of roof, placement of windows); Floor Plan (includes detailed dimensions of each room and the location of light fixtures, outlets, switches); Materials List (a complete summary of materials required including lumber, roofing, flooring and millwork); detailed Foundation, Framing and Roof plan. When applicable, all special construction (i.e., stairways, fireplaces, decks) are supplied in detail.

Working Drawings are available as a Single Set or as a 4-Set Package. Plan Costs are determined by square footage in the following three ways. (1) Under 1,000 square feet One Set is $30.00, Four-Set Package $65.00. (2) 1,000 to 1,800 square feet One Set is $35.00, Four-Set Package $70.00. (3) Over 1,800 Square Feet One Set is $40.00, Four-Set Package $75.00. Duplicate sets for all plans are available at $15.00 each. Mailing Costs: parcel post $1.50; air mail $3.00. Please compute price and send remittance by check or money order. If you wish you may charge your order to Mastercharge or BankAmericard by including your card number, expiration date and signature. With your order and remittance be certain to include your House Plan Number, quantity of sets and the ship-to address. All orders, remittances and inquiries should be directed to:

The Garlinghouse Co.,
Dept. OH-1,
Box 299,
320 S.W. 33rd St.,
Topeka, Kansas 66601

Addison	9098	Bakersfield	9310	Catskill	10188
Akron	320	Balsam	9237	Chaffee	164
Alamosa	9736	Barbary	10194	Chandler	9308
Allerton	316	Beachside	10056	Chapman	10210
Almonte	9684	Bellecoeur	10166	Chartrand	10128
Alyesbury	9115	Belleview	9970	Chateau	10026
Amesbury	9913	Berkely	158	Cheyenne	10148
Ancaster	9854	Biloxi	1012	Claycourt	9263
Annex One		Boswell	318	Collins	9213
Annex Two		Brandon	10176	Cortez	10022
Annex Three		Brighton	152	Craigmoor	314
Annex Four		Buckingham	10114		
Ardan	9312			Dallas	24012
Aries	9286	Capetown	236	Dartmouth	10004
Arroyo	9360	Carlenton	10190	Dartwood	10186
Ashland	10216	Carnaby	156	Dawnview	10054

De Land 9846	Girard 9290	Laurel 10222
Del Rio 9998	Gironde 9936	Leander 10024
Destry 1052	Glenview 9858	Le Land 9608
Devonport 9950	Granger 9294	Le Mans 9984
Donovan 122	Graycliff 20006	
Drayton 252	Graymoor 9278	MacVicar 10100
Dunbar 230		Madison 246
Durango 9838	Haddington 258	Maisland 9926
Durham 8266	Hampshire 9292	Mandano 10122
	Hancock 10164	Mandeville 10070
Eaglescroft 10204	Harrington 10162	Manitou 9870
Edgarton 1006	Hedgeston 9201	Manorfield 348
Elkwood 9876	Hedmark 9840	Mardale 1008
Empress 9042	Heiden 9900	Mattoon 270
Engleside 9167	Henerdon 9219	Maywood 166
Epernay 9986	Hermanas 10000	Medford 10016
Evanston 10082	Hershell 10172	Melville 148
	Highland 10002	Metcalf 374
Faemouth 9748	Highpoint 10058	Midland 358
Fairfield 9272	Holliver 10212	Midway 198
Falkland 10012	Holly 9734	Millington 9864
Fallbrook 9247		Millwright 10182
Faxon 9326	Irvingham 9584	Montclair 9269
Fenway 10102	Islay 9251	Moorhead 10214
Fernridge 6360		Morna 9754
Finsbury 9316	Kellam 9586	Morningside 9296
Flambeau 9592	Keltingham 10154	Mossridge 9382
Four Winds 10278	Keyport 202	
Foxridge 9812	Kristian 10160	Neptune 10178
		Neuchatel 9964
Gentle Oak 1056	Laughton 9235	New Orleans 24052

Northwood   9806

Oakengates   10006
Oakwood   370
Oldbury   9714
Olean   9032
Oliver   180
Osborn   9778

Parlington   9814
Pipkin   9818
Placid   10286
Plumwood   10282
Prescott   9828
Prospect   326

Quadella   9938
Quillan   9978
Quincy   9830
Quitman   9282

Ranchero   9594
Richland   5035

Richmond   10020
Robinson   9380
Rociada   10208
Rock Harbor   10280
Rowley   9942
Royce   9265
Roxanne   9958

Rustic   7664

Sagamore   10140
Sage   9288
St. Charles   9850
San Miguel   10146
San Souci   10064
Sena   9836
Shawano   9966
Shelton   9255
Sherrill   9094
Shoreham   9908
Sidney   10170
Sierra   10184
Skyline   9976
Smithston   274
Southwood   10098
Spanada   9956
Sporatan   9990
Sterling   184
Stinson   10284
Stoneville   9165
Stoneybrook   9225
Stovall   9046
Suburban   102
Suntown   334

Tahoe   10046
Telluride   10220
Terrymoor   330
Townsite   178

Trailtown   8110
Trenton   9266

Unberland   10200
Utrecht   9890

Valdosta   196
Vendome   9962
Viceroy   9762
Vickshire   9772
Vidalia   9906
Vienne   9878
Villa Bella   10174

Walden   10202
Wanchester   1058
Warner   9119
Watson   140
Wentworth   9332
Westchester   9896
Westmore   9048
Wheatridge   10196
Whitmark   9280
Willmar   9181
Woodson   9189
Worchester   9221
Wyman   10276

Yellowstone   9268
Youngstown   9852
Yvette   9882